KS3

ENGLISH
WORKBOOK

NICK BARBER

About this book

This workbook contains:

- topic-based questions for focused skills practice and to test your understanding of all the concepts on the Key Stage 3 course
- a test-style paper to ensure you are well prepared for end of key stage tests and assessments.

Key features

A Quick-fire, multiple-choice questions to get you warmed up.

C Longer, structured questions increase the demand and familiarise you with test-style questions.

At least two pages of practice for each topic.

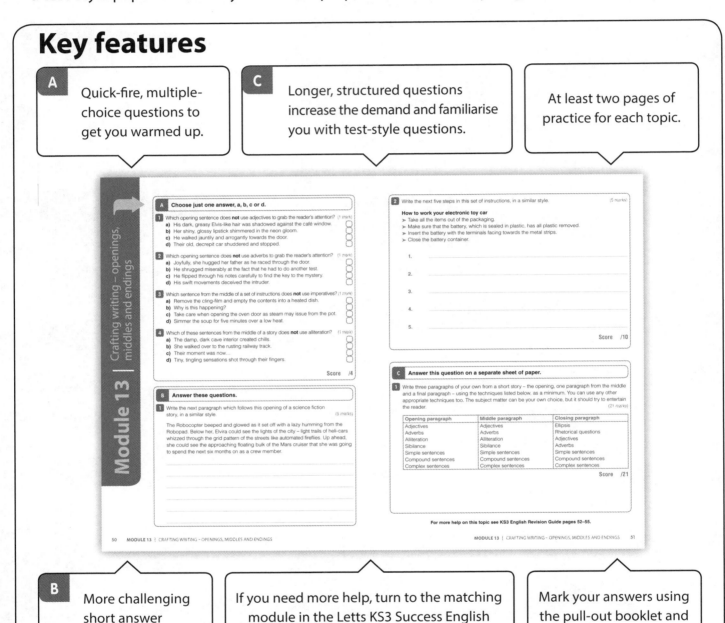

B More challenging short answer questions.

If you need more help, turn to the matching module in the Letts KS3 Success English Revision Guide (ISBN 9780008299149).

Mark your answers using the pull-out booklet and record your total scores.

ACKNOWLEDGEMENTS

The author and publisher are grateful to the copyright holders for permission to use quoted materials and images.

Images are ©Shutterstock.com

Every effort has been made to trace copyright holders and obtain their permission for the use of copyright material. The author and publisher will gladly receive information enabling them to rectify any error or omission in subsequent editions. All facts are correct at time of going to press.

Published by Letts Educational
An imprint of HarperCollinsPublishers
1 London Bridge Street
London SE1 9GF

ISBN: 9780008299156

Content first published 2014
This edition published 2018

10 9 8 7 6 5 4 3 2 1

© HarperCollinsPublishers Limited 2018

British Library Cataloguing in Publication Data.

A CIP record of this book is available from the British Library.

Commissioning Editor: Rebecca Skinner
Author: Nick Barber
Project Management: Fern Labram, Shelley Teasdale and Richard Toms
Editorial: Linda Mellor
Cover Design: Sarah Duxbury
Inside Concept Design: Paul Oates and Ian Wrigley
Production: Natalia Rebow
Text Design and Layout: Aptara®, Inc.
Printed in Great Britain by Martins the Printers

Contents

Read the two extracts and answer the questions that follow.

Extract 1

This extract is from *Romeo and Juliet* and it takes place at the Capulet ball, where Romeo sees and meets Juliet for the first time. This is their first conversation.

ROMEO (*To* **Juliet**)	If I profane with my unworthiest hand This holy shrine, the gentle sin is this: My lips, two blushing pilgrims, ready stand To smooth that rough touch with a tender kiss.
JULIET	Good pilgrim, you do wrong your hand too much, Which mannerly devotion shows in this; For saints have hands that pilgrims' hands do touch, And palm to palm is holy palmers' kiss.
ROMEO	Have not saints lips, and holy palmers too?
JULIET	Ay, pilgrim, lips that they must use in prayer.
ROMEO	O, then, dear saint, let lips do what hands do; They pray, grant thou, lest faith turn to despair.
JULIET	Saints do not move, though grant for prayers' sake.
ROMEO	Then move not, while my prayer's effect I take. (*They kiss*) Thus from my lips, by yours, my sin is purged.
JULIET	Then have my lips the sin that they have took.
ROMEO	Sin from thy lips? O trespass sweetly urged! Give me my sin again.
JULIET	You kiss by the book.

Extract 2

This extract is from *Much Ado About Nothing* where Benedick and Beatrice meet again. They used to be lovers, but parted on less than friendly terms. This passage is from where they speak for the first time since their parting.

BEATRICE	I wonder that you will still be talking, Signior Benedick – nobody marks you.
BENEDICK	What, my dear Lady Disdain! are you yet living?
BEATRICE	Is it possible disdain should die while she hath such meet food to feed it as Signior Benedick? Courtesy itself must convert to disdain, if you come in her presence.
BENEDICK	Then is courtesy a turncoat. But it is certain I am loved of all ladies, only you excepted: and I would I could find in my heart that I had not a hard heart; for, truly, I love none.
BEATRICE	A dear happiness to women: they would else have been troubled with a pernicious suitor. I thank God and my cold blood, I am of your humour for that: I had rather hear my dog bark at a crow than a man swear he loves me.
BENEDICK	God keep your ladyship still in that mind! so some gentleman or other shall 'scape a predestinate scratched face.
BEATRICE	Scratching could not make it worse, an 'twere such a face as yours were.
BENEDICK	Well, you are a rare parrot-teacher.
BEATRICE	A bird of my tongue is better than a beast of yours.
BENEDICK	I would my horse had the speed of your tongue, and so good a continuer. But keep your way, i' God's name; I have done.
BEATRICE	You always end with a jade's trick: I know you of old.

A — These questions are about Extract 1 from *Romeo and Juliet*. Choose just one answer, a, b, c or d.

1 Why does Romeo say that he has an "unworthiest hand"? (1 mark)
- a) He hasn't washed his hands before touching Juliet ◯
- b) He does not think he is of a high enough quality to even touch Juliet ◯
- c) He thinks that Juliet is of no value ◯
- d) He thinks that he is better than Juliet ◯

2 Which of these words, used by Romeo, is the odd one out? (1 mark)
- a) holy shrine ◯
- b) gentle sin ◯
- c) tender kiss ◯
- d) blushing pilgrims ◯

3 Which of these techniques is **not** present in this extract? (1 mark)
- a) imperatives ◯
- b) metaphors ◯
- c) rhetorical question ◯
- d) onomatopoeia ◯

4 From when Romeo first speaks to Juliet to when they kiss is 14 lines. Which kind of poem is this deliberately similar to? (1 mark)
- a) love sonnet ◯
- b) romantic ballad ◯
- c) love ode ◯
- d) lyric ◯

5 What does the line "Thus from my lips, by yours, my sin is purged" suggest? (1 mark)
- a) Romeo has become immortal by kissing Juliet ◯
- b) Romeo has made Juliet pure by kissing her ◯
- c) Romeo has had his sin removed by kissing Juliet ◯
- d) Romeo has forgotten about Rosaline by kissing Juliet ◯

Score /5

B — These questions are about Extract 1 from *Romeo and Juliet*. Answer all parts of each question.

1 What kind of imagery is used most often in this extract? (1 mark)

....

2 Pick out two examples of this kind of imagery and explain the effect of each one. (4 marks)

Example 1 ....

Explanation 1 ....

....

Example 2 ....

Explanation 2 ....

....

Score /5

C **Answer these questions about Extract 2 from *Much Ado About Nothing*.**

1 What does the phrase "But it is certain I / am loved of all ladies" suggest about Benedick? (2 marks)

....

....

....

....

2 Find one insult that Benedick uses on Beatrice and explain why it is effective. Use a quotation to support your answer. (2 marks)

....

....

....

....

3 Find one insult that Beatrice uses on Benedick and explain why it is effective. Use a quotation to support your answer. (2 marks)

....

....

....

....

4 Explain why Benedick wins this initial argument. Use a quotation or quotations to support your answer. (4 marks)

....

....

....

....

....

....

Score /10

For more help on this topic see KS3 English Revision Guide pages 4–7.

Read this extract from _Jane Eyre_ by Charlotte Brontë and answer the questions that follow. At this point in the story, the young Jane has been punished by being sent to the "Red Room" in her Aunt's house.

They went, shutting the door, and locking it behind them. The red-room was a square chamber, very seldom slept in, I might say never, indeed, unless when a chance influx of visitors at Gateshead Hall rendered it necessary to turn to account all the accommodation it contained: yet it was one of the largest and stateliest chambers in the mansion. A bed supported on massive pillars of mahogany, hung with curtains of deep red damask, stood out like a tabernacle in the centre; the two large windows, with their blinds always drawn down, were half shrouded in festoons and falls of similar drapery; the carpet was red; the table at the foot of the bed was covered with a crimson cloth; the walls were a soft fawn colour with a blush of pink in it; the wardrobe, the toilet-table, the chairs were of darkly polished old mahogany. Out of these deep surrounding shades rose high, and glared white, the piled-up mattresses and pillows of the bed, spread with a snowy Marseilles counterpane. Scarcely less prominent was an ample cushioned easy-chair near the head of the bed, also white, with a footstool before it; and looking, as I thought, like a pale throne. This room was chill, because it seldom had a fire; it was silent, because remote from the nursery and kitchen; solemn, because it was known to be so seldom entered. The house-maid alone came here on Saturdays, to wipe from the mirrors and the furniture a week's quiet dust: and Mrs. Reed herself, at far intervals, visited it to review the contents of a certain secret drawer in the wardrobe, where were stored divers parchments, her jewel-casket, and a miniature of her deceased husband; and in those last words lies the secret of the red-room — the spell which kept it so lonely in spite of its grandeur. Mr. Reed had been dead nine years: it was in this chamber he breathed his last; here he lay in state; hence his coffin was borne by the undertaker's men; and, since that day, a sense of dreary consecration had guarded it from frequent intrusion. My seat, to which Bessie and the bitter Miss Abbot had left me riveted, was a low ottoman near the marble chimney-piece; the bed rose before me; to my right hand there was the high, dark wardrobe, with subdued, broken reflections varying the gloss of its panels; to my left were the muffled windows; a great looking-glass between them repeated the vacant majesty of the bed and room. I was not quite sure whether they had locked the door; and when I dared move, I got up and went to see. Alas! yes: no jail was ever more secure. Returning, I had to cross before the looking- glass; my fascinated glance involuntarily explored the depth it revealed. All looked colder and darker in that visionary hollow than in reality: and the strange little figure there gazing at me, with a white face and arms specking the gloom, and glittering eyes of fear moving where all else was still, had the effect of a real spirit: I thought it like one of the tiny phantoms, half fairy, half imp, Bessie's evening stories represented as coming out of lone, ferny dells in moors, and appearing before the eyes of belated travellers. I returned to my stool. Superstition was with me at that moment; but it was not yet her hour for complete victory: my blood was still warm; the mood of the revolted slave was still bracing me with its bitter vigour; I had to stem a rapid rush of retrospective thought before I quailed to the dismal present. All John Reed's violent tyrannies, all his sisters' proud indifference, all his mother's aversion, all the servants' partiality, turned up in my disturbed mind like a dark deposit in a turbid well. Why was I always suffering, always browbeaten, always accused, for ever condemned? Why could I never please? Why was it useless to try to win any one's favour? Eliza, who was headstrong and selfish, was respected. Georgiana, who had a spoiled temper, a very acrid spite, a captious and insolent carriage, was universally indulged. Her beauty, her pink cheeks and golden curls, seemed to give delight to all who looked at her, and to purchase indemnity for every fault. John no one thwarted, much less punished; though he twisted the necks of the pigeons, killed the little pea-chicks, set the dogs at the sheep, stripped the hothouse vines of their fruit, and broke the buds off the choicest plants in the conservatory: he called his mother "old girl," too; sometimes reviled her for her dark skin, similar to his own; bluntly disregarded her wishes; not unfrequently tore and spoiled her silk attire; and he was still "her own darling." I dared commit no fault: I strove to fulfil every duty; and I was termed naughty and tiresome, sullen and sneaking, from morning to noon, and from noon to night.

A Choose just one answer, a, b, c or d.

1 What is "damask"? (1 mark)
- a) a kind of rare wood
- b) a kind of fabric
- c) a kind of glass
- d) a kind of ghost

2 What is an "ottoman"? (1 mark)
- a) a kind of padded seat
- b) a kind of bed
- c) a kind of ladder
- d) a fireplace

3 What does "consecration" mean in this passage? (1 mark)
- a) having a dull feeling
- b) having a spooky feeling
- c) something has been given religious respect
- d) something has been re-built

4 What does "indifference" mean in this passage? (1 mark)
- a) abuse
- b) torture
- c) pain
- d) not being bothered

5 What does "acrid" mean in this passage? (1 mark)
- a) unpleasantly bitter
- b) lacking in manners
- c) hot-tempered
- d) foul-mouthed

Score /5

B Answer all parts of each question.

1 Find two words that describe different shades of red. (2 marks)

2 Explain the different effects created by the two words that you chose in your answer to question 1. (2 marks)

Effect 1

Effect 2

Score /4

C Answer these questions.

1 Charlotte Brontë uses words and phrases to do with the supernatural to make this into a scary episode in the story. Find two quotations which show this and comment on how the words or phrases chosen create a scary mood.

(4 marks)

....

....

....

....

2 Charlotte Brontë also uses words and phrases to do with light and dark to create a scary mood. Find two quotations which show this and comment on how the words or phrases chosen create a scary mood.

(4 marks)

....

....

....

....

3 Charlotte Brontë also uses words to do with violence and pain to create a scary mood. Find two quotations which show this and comment on how the words chosen create a scary mood.

(4 marks)

....

....

....

....

4 Charlotte Brontë also uses words to do with size to create an intimidating mood. Find two quotations which show this and comment on how the words chosen create an intimidating mood.

(4 marks)

....

....

....

....

Score   /16

For more help on this topic see KS3 English Revision Guide pages 8–11.

Read the extract below from the opening of *Anne of Green Gables* by L.M. Montgomery and answer the questions that follow.

CHAPTER 1. Mrs. Rachel Lynde is Surprised

Mrs. Rachel Lynde lived just where the Avonlea main road dipped down into a little hollow, fringed with alders and ladies' eardrops and traversed by a brook that had its source away back in the woods of the old Cuthbert place; it was reputed to be an intricate, headlong brook in its earlier course through those woods, with dark secrets of pool and cascade; but by the time it reached Lynde's Hollow it was a quiet, well-conducted little stream, for not even a brook could run past Mrs. Rachel Lynde's door without due regard for decency and decorum; it probably was conscious that Mrs. Rachel was sitting at her window, keeping a sharp eye on everything that passed, from brooks and children up, and that if she noticed anything odd or out of place she would never rest until she had ferreted out the whys and wherefores thereof.

There are plenty of people in Avonlea and out of it, who can attend closely to their neighbour's business by dint of neglecting their own; but Mrs. Rachel Lynde was one of those capable creatures who can manage their own concerns and those of other folks into the bargain. She was a notable housewife; her work was always done and well done; she "ran" the Sewing Circle, helped run the Sunday-school, and was the strongest prop of the Church Aid Society and Foreign Missions Auxiliary. Yet with all this Mrs. Rachel found abundant time to sit for hours at her kitchen window, knitting "cotton warp" quilts—she had knitted sixteen of them, as Avonlea housekeepers were wont to tell in awed voices— and keeping a sharp eye on the main road that crossed the hollow and wound up the steep red hill beyond. Since Avonlea occupied a little triangular peninsula jutting out into the Gulf of St. Lawrence with water on two sides of it, anybody who went out of it or into it had to pass over that hill road and so run the unseen gauntlet of Mrs. Rachel's all-seeing eye.

She was sitting there one afternoon in early June. The sun was coming in at the window warm and bright; the orchard on the slope below the house was in a bridal flush of pinky-white bloom, hummed over by a myriad of bees. Thomas Lynde—a meek little man whom Avonlea people called "Rachel Lynde's husband"—was sowing his late turnip seed on the hill field beyond the barn; and Matthew Cuthbert ought to have been sowing his on the big red brook field away over by Green Gables. Mrs. Rachel knew that he ought because she had heard him tell Peter Morrison the evening before in William J. Blair's store over at Carmody that he meant to sow his turnip seed the next afternoon. Peter had asked him, of course, for Matthew Cuthbert had never been known to volunteer information about anything in his whole life.

And yet here was Matthew Cuthbert, at half-past three on the afternoon of a busy day, placidly driving over the hollow and up the hill; moreover, he wore a white collar and his best suit of clothes, which was plain proof that he was going out of Avonlea; and he had the buggy and the sorrel mare, which betokened that he was going a considerable distance. Now, where was Matthew Cuthbert going and why was he going there?

Had it been any other man in Avonlea, Mrs. Rachel, deftly putting this and that together, might have given a pretty good guess as to both questions. But Matthew so rarely went from home that it must be something pressing and unusual which was taking him; he was the shyest man alive and hated to have to go among strangers or to any place where he might have to talk. Matthew, dressed up with a white collar and driving in a buggy, was something that didn't happen often. Mrs. Rachel, ponder as she might, could make nothing of it and her afternoon's enjoyment was spoiled.

"I'll just step over to Green Gables after tea and find out from Marilla where he's gone and why," the worthy woman finally concluded. "He doesn't generally go to town this time of year and he NEVER visits; if he'd run out of turnip seed he wouldn't dress up and take the buggy to go for more; he wasn't driving fast enough to be going for a doctor. Yet something must have happened since last night to start him off. I'm clean puzzled, that's what, and I won't know a minute's peace of mind or conscience until I know what has taken Matthew Cuthbert out of Avonlea today."

Accordingly after tea Mrs. Rachel set out; she had not far to go; the big, rambling, orchard-embowered house where the Cuthberts lived was a scant quarter of a mile up the road from Lynde's Hollow. To be sure, the long lane made it a good deal further. Matthew Cuthbert's father, as shy and silent as his son after him, had got as far away as he possibly could from his fellow men without actually retreating into the woods when he founded his homestead. Green Gables was built at the furthest edge of his cleared land and there it was to this day, barely visible from the main road along which all the other Avonlea houses were so sociably situated. Mrs. Rachel Lynde did not call living in such a place LIVING at all.

A — Choose just one answer, a, b, c or d.

1 The first paragraph suggests that: (1 mark)
- **a)** Mrs Lynde is nosy ◯
- **b)** Mrs Lynde is clever ◯
- **c)** Mrs Lynde is wrong ◯
- **d)** Mrs Lynde is in charge of the stream ◯

2 The inverted commas in the phrase 'she "ran" the Sewing Circle' imply that: (1 mark)
- **a)** she was the leader of the sewing circle ◯
- **b)** she wasn't the leader of the sewing circle ◯
- **c)** she wasn't the leader of the sewing circle, but liked to think that she was ◯
- **d)** she couldn't sew ◯

3 Thomas Lynde is called "Rachel Lynde's husband" – what does this suggest? (1 mark)
- **a)** he controls his wife ◯
- **b)** he is very important ◯
- **c)** he is very proud of his wife ◯
- **d)** he doesn't have an identity of his own as his wife is too powerful ◯

4 Why is Rachel Lynde curious about Matthew Cuthbert? (1 mark)
- **a)** because he is leaving Avonlea and she doesn't understand why ◯
- **b)** because he is leaving Avonlea without her ◯
- **c)** because he is dressed up ◯
- **d)** because he hasn't visited her ◯

5 What does the last line "Mrs. Rachel Lynde did not call living in such a place LIVING at all" suggest? (1 mark)
- **a)** Rachel Lynde is shouting ◯
- **b)** Rachel Lynde is angry ◯
- **c)** Rachel Lynde thinks that the Cuthbert's house is impossible to enjoy living in ◯
- **d)** Rachel Lynde thinks that the Cuthbert's house is too close to the woods ◯

Score /5

B — Answer these questions.

1 Explain in your own words what this phrase suggests about the effect of the character of Rachel Lynde: "by the time it reached Lynde's Hollow it was a quiet, well-conducted little stream" (2 marks)

....

....

2 In this quotation, what does the word "ought" imply? "Matthew Cuthbert ought to have been sowing his on the big red brook field away over by Green Gables." (2 marks)

....

....

Score /4

C | Answer this question.

1 Look at the whole passage. Using four quotations, explain how L.M. Montgomery presents the character of Rachel Lynde. In your answer, try to read between the lines and explain how the quotations you pick out have more than one shade of meaning.

(8 marks)

....

....

....

....

....

....

....

....

....

....

....

....

....

....

....

....

....

....

Score   /8

For more help on this topic see KS3 English Revision Guide pages 12–15.

> **Read this passage from Charles Dickens' *Oliver Twist* and answer the questions that follow. It is set in a workhouse – these were unwelcoming places where poor people were sent to receive basic food and lodgings.**

The evening arrived; the boys took their places. The master, in his cook's uniform, stationed himself at the copper; his pauper assistants ranged themselves behind him; the gruel was served out; and a long grace was said over the short commons. The gruel disappeared; the boys whispered each other, and winked at Oliver; while his next neighbours nudged him. Child as he was, he was desperate with hunger, and reckless with misery. He rose from the table; and advancing to the master, basin and spoon in hand, said: somewhat alarmed at his own temerity:

'Please, sir, I want some more.'

The master was a fat, healthy man; but he turned very pale. He gazed in stupefied astonishment on the small rebel for some seconds, and then clung for support to the copper. The assistants were paralysed with wonder; the boys with fear.

'What!' said the master at length, in a faint voice.

'Please, sir,' replied Oliver, 'I want some more.'

The master aimed a blow at Oliver's head with the ladle; pinioned him in his arm; and shrieked aloud for the beadle.

The board were sitting in solemn conclave, when Mr. Bumble rushed into the room in great excitement, and addressing the gentleman in the high chair, said,

'Mr. Limbkins, I beg your pardon, sir! Oliver Twist has asked for more!'

There was a general start. Horror was depicted on every countenance.

'For *more*!' said Mr. Limbkins. 'Compose yourself, Bumble, and answer me distinctly. Do I understand that he asked for more, after he had eaten the supper allotted by the dietary?'

'He did, sir,' replied Bumble.

'That boy will be hung,' said the gentleman in the white waistcoat. 'I know that boy will be hung.'

Nobody controverted the prophetic gentleman's opinion. An animated discussion took place. Oliver was ordered into instant confinement; and a bill was next morning pasted on the outside of the gate, offering a reward of five pounds to anybody who would take Oliver Twist off the hands of the parish. In other words, five pounds and Oliver Twist were offered to any man or woman who wanted an apprentice to any trade, business, or calling.

'I never was more convinced of anything in my life,' said the gentleman in the white waistcoat, as he knocked at the gate and read the bill next morning: 'I never was more convinced of anything in my life, than I am that that boy will come to be hung.'

As I purpose to show in the sequel whether the white waistcoated gentleman was right or not, I should perhaps mar the interest of this narrative (supposing it to possess any at all), if I ventured to hint just yet, whether the life of Oliver Twist had this violent termination or no.

Choose just one answer, a, b, c or d.

1 What does "pauper" refer to in this extract? (1 mark)
   a) rich people
   b) skilled workers
   c) poor people
   d) chefs

2 What does "confinement" refer to in this passage? (1 mark)
   a) rest
   b) being locked up
   c) being chased
   d) being beaten

3 What would Charles Dickens **not** want his primary audience to do after reading this? (1 mark)
   a) laugh
   b) be shocked
   c) be alarmed
   d) be outraged

4 Which of these things was probably **not** Dickens' purpose in writing this extract? (1 mark)
   a) to criticise the amount of food in workhouses
   b) to show the greed of children in workhouses
   c) to show the level of violence in workhouses
   d) to show the lack of compassion in workhouses

5 This extract is at the end of a chapter. Why does Dickens end on a cliffhanger? (1 mark)
   a) he was writing in instalments and wanted readers to buy the next edition
   b) he wanted to intrigue the readers
   c) he wanted to gain sympathy for Oliver Twist's fate
   d) all of these

6 How might Dickens have used this novel to affect public opinion about workhouses? (1 mark)
   a) he realised that he couldn't change anything
   b) he hoped that they would be entertained by them and find them funny
   c) he hoped that they would be shocked by his writing and ask for change
   d) he hoped that they would be impressed by what was happening in them

7 *Oliver Twist* originally appeared in instalments in 1837, before being published as a book. How might this have helped to raise awareness of problems in workhouses? (1 mark)
   a) between instalments, people had time to talk about what they had read
   b) between instalments, people's anger and concern built up
   c) neither of these
   d) both a) and b)

Score /7

B   Answer these questions.

1 How does the phrase "'Please, sir, I want some more.'" Get the audience's
sympathy? Give two reasons.   (2 marks)

....

....

....

....

....

2 Why might Charles Dickens have included this sentence in the incident? "The
master aimed a blow at Oliver's head with the ladle; pinioned him in his arm;
and shrieked aloud for the beadle." Give three reasons.   (3 marks)

....

....

....

....

....

....

3 What is the purpose of the final paragraph?   (2 marks)

....

....

....

....

....

Score   /7

C | Answer these questions.

1 How does Charles Dickens use sentence and clause lengths to influence the reader?
Give three examples and back up your ideas with quotations. (6 marks)

....

....

....

....

....

....

....

2 How does Charles Dickens use verbs to both shock the audience and to build up tension?
Give two examples and back up your ideas with quotations. (4 marks)

....

....

....

....

....

3 Explain in your own words what the effects of this passage might have been on rich and
poor Victorian readers. Give four effects. (4 marks)

....

....

....

....

....

....

Score   /14

For more help on this topic see KS3 English Revision Guide pages 16–19.

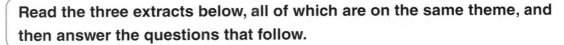

Read the three extracts below, all of which are on the same theme, and then answer the questions that follow.

Extract 1

This extract is from *Romeo and Juliet* Act 2 Scene 2. Romeo is hiding below Juliet's window, waiting to catch sight of her.

JULIET	Ay me!
ROMEO	She speaks: O, speak again, bright angel! for thou art As glorious to this night, being o'er my head As is a winged messenger of heaven Unto the white-upturned wondering eyes Of mortals that fall back to gaze on him When he bestrides the lazy-pacing clouds And sails upon the bosom of the air.
JULIET	O Romeo, Romeo! wherefore art thou Romeo? Deny thy father and refuse thy name Or, if thou wilt not, be but sworn my love, And I'll no longer be a Capulet.
ROMEO (*Aside*)	Shall I hear more, or shall I speak at this?
JULIET	'Tis but thy name that is my enemy; Thou art thyself, though not a Montague. What's Montague? it is nor hand, nor foot, Nor arm, nor face, nor any other part Belonging to a man. O, be some other name! What's in a name? that which we call a rose By any other name would smell as sweet;

Extract 2

This extract is from Jane Austen's *Pride and Prejudice*. Elizabeth Bennet, after refusing to marry Mr Darcy initially, has now seen the error of her ways, but does not know how she will be able to speak to him again.

She was in hopes that the evening would afford some opportunity of bringing them together; that the whole of the visit would not pass away without enabling them to enter into something more of conversation than the mere ceremonious salutation attending his entrance. Anxious and uneasy, the period which passed in the drawing-room, before the gentlemen came, was wearisome and dull to a degree that almost made her uncivil. She looked forward to their entrance as the point on which all her chance of pleasure for the evening must depend.

"If he does not come to me, *then*," said she, "I shall give him up for ever."

The gentlemen came; and she thought he looked as if he would have answered her hopes; but, alas! the ladies had crowded round the table, where Miss Bennet was making tea, and Elizabeth pouring out the coffee, in so close a confederacy that there was not a single vacancy near her which would admit of a chair. And on the gentlemen's approaching, one of the girls moved closer to her than ever, and said, in a whisper:

"The men shan't come and part us, I am determined. We want none of them; do we?"

Darcy had walked away to another part of the room. She followed him with her eyes, envied everyone to whom he spoke, had scarcely patience enough to help anybody to coffee; and then was enraged against herself for being so silly!

"A man who has once been refused! How could I ever be foolish enough to expect a renewal of his love? Is there one among the sex, who would not protest against such a weakness as a second proposal to the same woman? There is no indignity so abhorrent to their feelings!"

Extract 3

This is a poem called "I hid my love" by John Clare, who lived from 1793–1864.

I hid my love when young till I

Couldn't bear the buzzing of a fly;

I hid my love to my despite

Till I could not bear to look at light;

I dare not gaze upon her face

But left her memory in each place;

Where'er I saw a wild flower lie

I kissed and bade my love goodbye.

I met her in the greenest dells,

Where dewdrops pearl the wood bluebells;

The lost breeze kissed her bright blue eye,

The bee kissed and went singing by,

A sunbeam found a passage there,

A gold chain round her neck so fair;

As secret as the wild bee's song

She lay there all the summer long.

I hid my love in field and town

Till e'en the breeze would knock me down;

The bees seemed singing ballads o'er,

The fly's bass turned to lion's roar;

And even the silence found a tongue,

To haunt me all the summer long;

The riddle nature could not prove

Was nothing else but secret love.

A   Choose just one answer, a, b, c or d.

1 Which extract allows us to see the loving thoughts of more than one character? (1 mark)
a) extract 1 ◯
b) extract 2 ◯
c) extract 3 ◯
d) all of them ◯

2 Which genre features do all of these texts share? (1 mark)
a) action ◯
b) adventure ◯
c) mystery ◯
d) romance ◯

3 Which of these extracts is written in the third person? (1 mark)
a) extract 1 ◯
b) extract 2 ◯
c) extract 3 ◯
d) all of them ◯

4 Which of these extracts was written with the intention of it being performed? (1 mark)
a) extract 1 ◯
b) extract 2 ◯
c) extract 3 ◯
d) all of them ◯

5 Which of these extracts uses the least figurative language to put over loving thoughts? (1 mark)
a) extract 1 ◯
b) extract 2 ◯
c) extract 3 ◯
d) extracts 1 and 3 ◯

Score   /5

B   Answer these questions.

1 Give two ways that the form of Extract 1 is different from Extracts 2 and 3. (2 marks)

....

....

....

....

2 Extract 2 is from a prose novel. Explain two advantages that this gives the writer in this text. (2 marks)

....

....

....

....

Score   /4

C · Answer this question.

1 All three extracts deal with the difficulty of declaring feelings for someone. Find a quotation from each extract and explain how each extract deals with this issue in different ways. (6 marks)

Score /6

For more help on this topic see KS3 English Revision Guide pages 20–23.

> **Read the extract from *The Pied Piper of Hamelin* by Robert Browning and answer the questions that follow.**

Verse 1

Hamelin Town's in Brunswick,

By famous Hanover city;

The river Weser, deep and wide,

Washes its wall on the southern side;

A pleasanter spot you never spied;

But, when begins my ditty,

Almost five hundred years ago,

To see the townsfolk suffer so

From vermin, was a pity.

Verse 2

Rats!

They fought the dogs and killed the cats,

And bit the babies in the cradles,

And ate the cheeses out of the vats,

And licked the soup from the cooks' own ladles,

Split open the kegs of salted sprats,

Made nests inside men's Sunday hats,

And even spoiled the women's chats,

By drowning their speaking

With shrieking and squeaking

In fifty different sharps and flats.

Verse 3

At last the people in a body

To the Town Hall came flocking:

"Tis clear," cried they, "our Mayor's a noddy;

"And as for our Corporation – shocking

"To think we buy gowns lined with ermine

"For dolts that can't or won't determine

"What's best to rid us of our vermin!

"You hope, because you're old and obese,

"To find in the furry civic robe ease?

"Rouse up, sirs! Give your brains a racking

"To find the remedy we're lacking,

"Or, sure as fate, we'll send you packing!"

At this the Mayor and Corporation

Quaked with a mighty consternation.

1 In verse 1, how many lines rhyme with (but not including) the first one? (1 mark)
a) none
b) one
c) two
d) three

2 What is the rhyme pattern of verse 1? (1 mark)
a) ABCABCABC
b) ABCCCBDDB
c) ABDDDCAAC
d) ABCDDBAAB

3 In verse 2, how many lines rhyme with (but not including) the first one? (1 mark)
a) four
b) five
c) six
d) seven

4 What is the rhyme pattern of verse 2? (1 mark)
a) ABABAAACCAA
b) AABABAAACCA
c) ACABACABAAB
d) ABBACCCBBAB

5 What is the main effect of the change in rhyme pattern from verse 1 to verse 2? (1 mark)
a) verse 2 becomes calmer
b) verse 2 becomes duller
c) verse 2 becomes more frantic
d) verse 2 becomes more realistic

6 How many syllables are there in the lines in these verses? (1 mark)
a) between 1 and 10, depending on the line
b) between 6 and 10, depending on the line
c) between 7 and 10, depending on the line
d) between 8 and 10, depending on the line

7 What is the effect on the rhythm, of the four lines in verse 2 starting with "And"? (1 mark)
a) they slow the poem down
b) they speed the poem up
c) they make the poem duller
d) they make the poem clearer

Score   /7

B **Answer these questions.**

1 In verse three, find two ways that the writer Robert Browning increases the pace and affects the tone of the poem, using rhythm and/or rhyme.

Write two quotations below and explain how one of your examples increases the poem's pace and how the other changes the poem's tone. (4 marks)

....

....

....

....

....

....

....

....

....

....

2 Verse 3 ends on a rhyming couplet – what is the effect of this? (2 marks)

....

....

....

....

Score /6

C Answer these questions.

1 Using quotations to support your answer, explain how Robert Browning has used rhythm and/or rhyme in this poem to make it suitable for children.

(6 marks)

....

....

....

....

....

....

....

....

....

....

2 Using quotations to support your answer, explain how Robert Browning uses alliteration to affect the pace and/or tone of the poem.

(4 marks)

....

....

....

....

....

....

....

Score   /10

For more help on this topic see KS3 English Revision Guide pages 24–27.

A   Choose just one answer, a, b, c or d.

1 Which of these is **not** a type of poem?   (1 mark)
  a) sonnet
  b) limerick
  c) acrostic
  d) restoration comedy

2 Which of these is the most likely to contain imaginative writing?   (1 mark)
  a) a story
  b) a dictionary
  c) an instruction manual
  d) a forensic report

3 Which of these is least likely to be a form of imaginative writing?   (1 mark)
  a) a novel
  b) a personal description
  c) a cookery book
  d) a poem

4 Which of these is **not** a form of imaginative verse?   (1 mark)
  a) ballad
  b) free verse
  c) limerick
  d) novella

5 Which of these is **not** a type of play?   (1 mark)
  a) pantomime
  b) farce
  c) rune
  d) tragedy

6 Which of these genres is least likely to include imaginative writing?   (1 mark)
  a) informative writing
  b) horror writing
  c) romance writing
  d) comedy writing

7 Which of these is **not** an advantage of writing in the first person?   (1 mark)
  a) it is easier to create empathy with a character
  b) there is a distance between reader and character
  c) it allows the reader directly into a character's thoughts
  d) it allows the character to explain themselves

Score   /7

1 Complete the passage below. The writer's intention is to create a spooky, mysterious feeling, so the words that you place in the gaps should all help to create that mood. You should not repeat a word, even if it is a good one. There are several ways that you might do this. (10 marks)

Bill walked .... to the .... door.

The .... house in front of him made him feel ....

Little did he know what .... things lay inside, lurking ....

in the .... dark, waiting for someone like him to arrive.

He .... pushed the door open and stepped .... inside.

From the darkness he heard a .... sound.

2 Now complete the passage again, but this time the writer's intention is to create a happy feeling, so the words that you place in the gaps should all help to create that mood. You should not repeat a word, even if it is a good one. There are several ways that you might do this. (10 marks)

Bill walked .... to the .... door.

The .... house in front of him made him feel ....

Little did he know what .... things lay inside, lurking ....

in the .... dark, waiting for someone like him to arrive.

He .... pushed the door open and stepped .... inside.

From the darkness he heard a .... sound.

3 Now complete the passage once again, but this time the writer's intention is to create a warm, summery feeling, so the words that you place in the gaps should all help to create that mood. You should not repeat a word, even if it is a good one. There are several ways that you might do this. (10 marks)

Bill walked .... to the .... door.

The .... house in front of him made him feel ....

Little did he know what .... things lay inside, lurking ....

in the .... dark, waiting for someone like him to arrive.

He .... pushed the door open and stepped .... inside.

From the darkness he heard a .... sound.

Score **/30**

C Answer this question.

1 Write an extended piece of prose description; five paragraphs about a place that you disliked. The brief for the writing is as follows:

➤ It should be written in the third person.
➤ It should contain a range of unusual vocabulary for effect.
➤ It should have a range of simple, compound and complex sentences for effect.
➤ It should be aimed at a teenage reader.
➤ It should be written in a genre-style that appeals to teenage readers.
➤ It should include both the active and passive voice.

Before you start to write, use the space below to plan your ideas. Make notes on what you are going to put in each paragraph and where you might include all the bullet points above.

(6 marks)

Planning box

Write your five paragraphs here. Continue on a separate sheet if needed.

For more help on this topic see KS3 English Revision Guide pages 28–31.

A Choose just one answer, a, b, c or d.

1 Which of these is **not** a feature of formal writing? (1 mark)
   a) the writing needs to be clear
   b) it needs to be as imaginative as possible
   c) it needs to be well-structured and organised
   d) it needs vocabulary suitable for its audience

2 Which of these is **not** a type of formal writing? (1 mark)
   a) business letter
   b) job application
   c) melodrama
   d) report

3 Which of these is **not** appropriate when starting a formal letter? (1 mark)
   a) Hiya
   b) Dear Sir
   c) To whom it may concern
   d) Dear Mrs Jones

4 Which of these is appropriate in a formal letter? (1 mark)
   a) Hello m8
   b) Hiya mate
   c) Dear Sir
   d) Thanks – LOL

5 Which of these is appropriate when writing a formal letter? (1 mark)
   a) slang
   b) using the nickname of the person you are writing to
   c) addressing the recipient by their title and surname, i.e. Mrs Wardle
   d) ending with "love from"

6 Which of these is **not** appropriate in a formal letter? (1 mark)
   a) Thanking you in anticipation
   b) It has come to my attention
   c) You've gotta be kidding?
   d) With regard to your previous letter

7 Which of these is **not** a feature of a formal letter? (1 mark)
   a) an address to which you are writing
   b) a date
   c) an appropriately informal salutation
   d) an appropriately formal ending

Score /7

B Answer this question.

1 Read this letter content which has been written in an informal style. Change it to a more formal style, but keeping the same facts and information. There are several ways that this might be done.

(1 mark)

Hi Baz,

Soz – I wasn't able to get to your business lunch last Friday. I was really looking forward to it and I was all ready to leave the house when my sis arrived at the house for a surprise visit!! She was only around for the one evening before she went to my bro's house so I had to stay with her. Soz Baz!

I tried to ring you but your phone was busy when I rang. Then I was out with my sis in town and didn't have the chance to ring again. D'oh.

Laters?
Wazza

Score   /1

c   Answer this question.

1 Write a letter of complaint, using the following information. You need to include all of the following information appropriately in your letter and write in an appropriately formal style.

Layout information
➤ Your address – 30, Northumberland Avenue, Stokely, Stanfordshire, SA11 6LP
➤ An address to which you are writing – Complaints Department, Small Cameras Ltd
➤ The date when you wrote the letter – 26 January 2015
➤ An appropriately formal salutation
➤ An appropriately formal ending/closing

Content information
You are complaining about a camera that you bought. It does not work as advertised. It clicks when the button is pressed but does not record images to its memory card. You are an experienced photographer, so you know that you have not mis-read the instructions.

The camera cost £1000, so you are anxious to get a replacement or your money back. You would also like compensation for loss of earnings as you had to turn down a photo-shoot worth £250 when the camera did not work.

Style information
➤ Your tone should be firm, persuasive and factual, but not offensive.
➤ Use short sentences to explain the problem.
➤ Use longer sentences to develop your complaint and explain how you would like it resolved.

Write the letter on the page opposite.   (10 marks)

For more help on this topic see KS3 English Revision Guide pages 32–35.

A Choose just one answer, a, b, c or d.

1 Which of these is likely to be an advantage of planning in your head? (1 mark)
- **a)** it is quick and easy
- **b)** it suits longer answers
- **c)** it is good for complex answers
- **d)** not good for short answers

2 Which of these is unlikely to be an advantage of making lists? (1 mark)
- **a)** easy to make ideas chronological
- **b)** easy to make ideas sequential
- **c)** easy to plan the sequence of an argument from
- **d)** good for cross-referencing ideas

3 Which of these is **not** usually a way of ordering ideas in a spider diagram? (1 mark)
- **a)** numbering
- **b)** colour-coding
- **c)** lists
- **d)** highlighting

4 Which of these is **not** usually a way of ordering ideas in a mind-map? (1 mark)
- **a)** lines showing the flow of ideas
- **b)** colour coding
- **c)** lists
- **d)** highlighting

5 Which of these things is **not** usually an advantage of using sticky notes to organise ideas? (1 mark)
- **a)** ability to re-arrange ideas
- **b)** ability to remove and replace ideas
- **c)** ability to work collaboratively
- **d)** ability to cut and paste straight to a computer

6 Which of these is **not** true about paragraphs? (1 mark)
- **a)** they must have six lines in them
- **b)** they can be of different lengths
- **c)** short ones might be used to show shock
- **d)** long ones might be used to add detail

7 Which of these is **not** true about writing a conclusion? (1 mark)
- **a)** it could be used to sum up
- **b)** it could be used to end on a cliff-hanger
- **c)** it could be used to evaluate
- **d)** it could be used to introduce your main ideas

Score /7

Answer these questions.

1 Re-arrange the paragraph plan in this chart so that it makes sense. (5 marks)

Paragraph topics – not in order	Paragraph topics – in order
First character finds mysterious object	
Set the scene for the story	
Deadly ray stuns first character	
Bring first character into the scene	
Mysterious object gives off deadly ray	

2 Re-arrange the paragraph plan in this table so that it makes sense. (5 marks)

Paragraph topics – not in order	Paragraph topics – in order
Explain how ingredients are to be prepared	
Explain, while ingredients are cooking, how dishes need to be warmed ready for fully cooked ingredients	
Explain ingredients needed for recipe	
Explain how cooked ingredients need to be presented on warmed dishes	
Explain how ingredients are cooked	

3 Re-arrange the paragraph plan in this chart so that it makes sense. (5 marks)

Paragraph topics – not in order	Paragraph topics – in order
Paragraph stating the purpose of writing	
Opening salutation for the letter	
Paragraph concluding the main body of the letter	
Paragraph developing the opening point	
Closing for the letter	

Score /15

C **Answer the following question.**

1 The remainder of this module is divided into four sections. To discover which planning approach suits you best, plan an answer to the task below, using each of the four planning types. When you have done it, look at all four plans and see which has produced the best plan for you to write up an answer. (4 marks)

Task – Write a description of a place that has had a big effect on you.

1. Planning in your head

2. Make lists

3. Spider diagram

4. Mind-map

Score   /4

For more help on this topic see KS3 English Revision Guide pages 36–39.

A | **Choose just one answer, a, b, c or d.**

1 Which of these publications is best suited to simple vocabulary and sentences? *(1 mark)*
- **a)** an adult horror novel
- **b)** a technical machinery manual for experts
- **c)** a young child's story book
- **d)** an article in a business newspaper

2 Which of these publications is best suited to slang, informal vocabulary and style? *(1 mark)*
- **a)** a tourist information guide book
- **b)** a teenage magazine
- **c)** a Sunday newspaper investigative report
- **d)** a financial article in a daily newspaper

3 Which of these is likely to be the most formal in style? *(1 mark)*
- **a)** a teenage magazine letters page
- **b)** a young children's comic
- **c)** a set of instructions for a complex piece of machinery
- **d)** a science-fiction novel

4 Which of these phrases would suit a holiday brochure? *(1 mark)*
- **a)** the hotel is rubbish
- **b)** the hotel is splendidly situated
- **c)** the hotel is ace
- **d)** the hotel is well nice

5 Which of these phrases would suit a camera instruction manual? *(1 mark)*
- **a)** press the shutter release
- **b)** give it some welly
- **c)** plonk it down slowly
- **d)** fiddle with it a bit

6 Which of these statements is **not** true about secondary audiences? *(1 mark)*
- **a)** the writer knows exactly who they are
- **b)** the writer does not know exactly who they are
- **c)** they can be a range of people
- **d)** they could be anyone who reads a text

7 Which of these is a reason to write a novel? *(1 mark)*
- **a)** to make money
- **b)** to entertain
- **c)** to rebel against the style of earlier novels
- **d)** all three of these

Score /7

B **Answer these questions.**

1 Here are a number of sentences from a formal letter. Change them so that they become more informal and personal. These can be re-written in a variety of ways, but the first one is done for you as an example of what you might do.

Formal – I would like to request your company this evening.

Informal – Are you coming out with me tonight?

Complete the table below.

(5 marks)

Formal	Would you do me the honour of going shopping with me?
Informal	
Formal	Henceforth I shall be known as Ernest Tubb.
Informal	
Formal	Would you deny me the opportunity to visit my mother?
Informal	
Formal	The accommodation would have benefited from sanitary improvement.
Informal	
Formal	I would like to request that you desist.
Informal	

2 Write a short e-mail to a friend, using an informal style. You must use all the words and phrases in the table once. There are several ways that this might be done.

(8 marks)

Hi!	as daft as a soggy brush
You've gotta be joking?	I'm not bothered
Bye bye for now	a load of twaddle
crikey	Cor blimey!

Score **/13**

c   Answer these questions.

1 Using the information in the table below, write the opening two paragraphs for a science fiction story aimed at teenagers.   (6 marks)

The writing should reflect, or include, the following:

Futuristic sounding names	New technology
A fast-paced, descriptive first paragraph, to grab attention	Rhetorical questions, to ask the reader "What if?"
A futuristic or alien setting	A second paragraph which introduces a main character

2 Using the information in the table below, write a page for a cookery book aimed at students who are cooking for themselves for probably the first time.

(6 marks)

The writing should reflect, or include, the following:

Straightforward vocabulary	Headings and sections
Chatty style	Simple and compound sentences
Lists of ingredients and numbered instructions	Assume that the equipment being used is very basic and the skill levels of the reader are also low.

Score /12

For more help on this topic see KS3 English Revision Guide pages 40–43.

A Choose just one answer, a, b, c or d.

1 Which of these is **not** a non-narrative text? (1 mark)
a) a shopping list ◯
b) a letter requesting information ◯
c) a novel ◯
d) a technical manual ◯

2 Which of these is a feature of a non-narrative text? (1 mark)
a) it tells a story ◯
b) it can deal with things in alphabetical order or in sections ◯
c) animals are given human attributes ◯
d) it has a plot ◯

3 Which non-narrative text might include sections on ingredients and recipes? (1 mark)
a) a car manual ◯
b) a Christmas shopping list ◯
c) a cookery book ◯
d) a dictionary ◯

4 Which non-narrative text might include sections on engines and machinery? (1 mark)
a) a car manual ◯
b) a Christmas shopping list ◯
c) a cookery book ◯
d) a dictionary ◯

5 Which non-narrative text will most likely be in alphabetical order? (1 mark)
a) a car manual ◯
b) a Christmas shopping list ◯
c) a cookery book ◯
d) a dictionary ◯

Score /5

B Answer this question.

1 Here are a set of entries for an encyclopaedia. Organise them in alphabetical order, in the order that they should appear. (9 marks)

Dogs	Vultures	Sparrows
Cats	Chickens	Lizards
Lions	Tigers	Elephants

1	
2	
3	
4	
5	
6	
7	
8	
9	

Score /9

READING

Module 1: Shakespeare (pages 6–7)

A

1. b **2.** c **3.** d **4.** a **5.** c

B

1. Religious/spiritual imagery
2. Several answers are possible. These could include (in any order): holy shrine (Romeo worships Juliet)/gentle sin (The effect of Romeo's kiss)/two blushing pilgrims (refers to his lips and his embarrassment)/pilgrim (Romeo is on a journey to worship Juliet)/mannerly devotion (implies that Romeo is paying appropriate attention to Juliet)/saints have hands that pilgrims' hands do touch (Juliet implies that they are behaving in a holy manner, like saints)/palm to palm is holy palmers' kiss (praying hands are joined like lips)/Have not saints lips, and holy palmers too (Romeo is making a link between praying and kissing)/Lips that they must use in prayer (Juliet is hinting that kissing is a form of worship)/dear saint, let lips do what hands do (Romeo extends Juliet's comparison and is suggesting they kiss)/my prayer's effect I take (Romeo says he'll kiss Juliet)/from my lips, by yours, my sin is purged (the kiss seals the start of their relationship)/references to "sin" (the act of kissing)
(1 mark for each example and explanation)

C

1. Answers might include – he is self-confident/arrogant/a joker/likes to wind people up
(1 mark for each)
2. Several answers possible, which might include – my dear lady Disdain! are you yet living (he can't believe that someone so miserable or stuck up is still alive)/...so some gentleman or other shall 'scape a predestinate scratched face (he implies that Beatrice is like an animal)/A rare parrot teacher (he implies that she has nothing better to do than repeat rubbish)/I would my horse had the speed of your tongue (he implies that she never shuts up and keeps talking)
(1 mark for quotation and 1 mark for explanation)
3. Several answers possible, which might include – nobody marks you (nobody pays any attention to you)/ Is it possible disdain should die…if you come in her presence (Beatrice is suggesting that Benedick has a poisonous personality)/A dear happiness to women: they would else have been troubled with a pernicious suitor (Beatrice implies that women are better off without the likes of Benedick and should be glad that he doesn't love any of them)/Scratching could not make it worse….as yours were (she's saying his face/ appearance couldn't be worse if it was scratched)/A bird of my tongue is better than a beast of yours (she's implying that she may have faults, but she'd rather have them, than be like him)
(1 mark for quotation and 1 mark for explanation)
4. The end of the extract shows that Beatrice admits that Benedick wins the argument as he manages to get the last word – But keep your way, i' God's name; I have done/**BEATRICE** You always end with a jade's trick: I know you of old. "You always end with a jade's trick" implies that he has cheated to win the argument.
(2 marks for explanation and 2 marks for supporting quotation(s))

Module 2: Building vocabulary through reading (pages 10–11)

A

1. b **2.** a **3.** c **4.** d **5.** a

B

1. Answers will include – deep red/crimson/blush of pink/ pink cheeks
(1 mark for each)
2. Answers can be in any order for Effect 1 or Effect 2. Deep red (luxurious)/crimson (luxurious and rich, reminiscent of blood)/blush of pink (a hint of redness, almost reflecting the rest of the room, touched by it)/ pink cheeks (healthy and lively)
(1 mark for each)

C

1. Various answers possible. Most likely suggestions include – here he lay in state….frequent intrusion (implies that it was a death scene that hadn't been revisited)/the strange little figure there gazing at me….. had the effect of a real spirit (her own reflection is described like a ghost)
(1 mark for each quotation and 1 mark for each supporting comment)
2. Various answers possible. Most likely suggestions include – blinds always drawn down (no light or life enters)/darkly polished old mahogany (creates a feeling of age)/dark wardrobe (tall, ominous furniture – what's inside?)/white face and arms specking the gloom (gives the impression of a ghost/spirit in the darkness)
(1 mark for each quotation and 1 mark for each supporting comment)
3. Various answers possible. Most likely suggestions include – All John Reed's violent tyrannies, all his sisters' proud indifference, all his mother's aversion, all the servants' partiality, turned up in my disturbed mind like a dark deposit in a turbid well (gives a feeling of being bullied and wanting to react against it)/John no one thwarted, much less punished; though he twisted the necks of the pigeons, killed the little pea-chicks, set the dogs at the sheep, stripped the hothouse vines of their fruit, and broke the buds off the choicest plants in the conservatory (gives the impression that he is a terrible bully, through the amount of language)
(1 mark for each quotation and 1 mark for each supporting comment)
4. Various answers possible. Most likely suggestions include – one of the largest and stateliest chambers in the mansion. A bed supported on massive pillars of mahogany (the room is large and intimidating to the young Jane)/Out of these deep surrounding shades rose high (the room's contents are intimidating to the small young girl)
(1 mark for each quotation and 1 mark for each supporting comment)

Module 3: Reading between the lines (pages 14–15)

A

1. a **2.** c **3.** d **4.** a **5.** c

B

1. It implies that the stream had got smaller *(1 mark)* and that it is almost having to change because Rachel Lynde is almost powerful and bossy enough to make it change *(1 mark)*.

2. He is not behaving how Rachel Lynde feels that he should *(1 mark)*, according to the way that she sees patterns of behaviour in the village *(1 mark)*.

C

1. Various answers possible. The quotations can be in any order and might include the following: not even a brook could run past Mrs. Rachel Lynde's door without due regard for decency and decorum (implies that she is so nosy that even nature has to behave in front of her)/Mrs. Rachel Lynde was one of those capable creatures who can manage their own concerns and those of other folks into the bargain (implies that she has a high opinion of herself and her worth and messes in other people's business)/She was a notable housewife; her work was always done and well done (appearances are important to her – she needs to be seen doing the "right" things)/Yet with all this Mrs. Rachel found abundant time to sit for hours at her kitchen window (she gives the impression of being busy, but may well not be – and again, is quite nosy)
(1 mark for each explanation and 1 mark for each supporting quotation)

Module 4: Effect of audience, purpose and context (pages 17–19)

A

1. c **2.** b **3.** a **4.** b **5.** d **6.** c **7.** d

B

1. By using good manners, (Please, sir) Oliver's character gains more sympathy when he is rudely answered. The short sentence "I want some more" might imply a very direct and honest request – he must be desperate if this is compared to the "gruel" he has to eat.
(1 mark for each reason)

2. The use of the "ladle" implies the violence is sudden and not thought out, as the nearest object has been grabbed./"pinioned" is a strong word to use – out of proportion violence to the simple request of Oliver/shrieked aloud for the beadle (over-exaggerated response to what Oliver has asked for – more sympathy for Oliver, less for the master)
(1 mark for each reason)

3. Dickens is not giving the end of the incident away, as he wants to keep the audience waiting, as he probably wanted them to buy the next instalment. He wants the audience to be in suspense. He also is playing down whether the fate of Oliver has any interest – making the reader question their own values.
(1 mark for each purpose up to a maximum of 2)

C

1. Various answers possible. These might include – short sentences, e.g. There was a general start. Horror was depicted on every countenance. (Creates a mood of shock) / Short sentences like 'For more!' said Mr. Limbkins. (To show outrage and anger) / Complex sentences to add description, e.g. Child as he was, he was desperate with hunger, and reckless with misery (creates a feeling of sympathy for Oliver's situation)
(1 mark for each example and 1 mark for each supporting quotation)

2. Various answers possible. These might include – He gazed in stupefied astonishment on the small rebel for some seconds, and then clung for support to the copper. The assistants were paralysed with wonder; the boys with fear. (Verbs create tension as the reader is held in suspense by the actions of the master)/The master aimed a blow at Oliver's head with the ladle; pinioned him in his arm; and shrieked aloud for the beadle. (Violent verbs show the ferocity of the attack)
(1 mark for each example and 1 mark for each supporting quotation)

3. Various answers possible. Effects on the rich – shock at what was going on in the workhouses./Some might agree with the actions of the master, to keep poor people in their place. Understanding of a way of life that they knew little about. Effects on the poor – empathy with Oliver/Shock at the violence/Sympathy with Oliver's poor status and hunger.
(1 mark for each)

Module 5: Language, form and meaning (pages 22–23)

A

1. d **2.** d **3.** b **4.** a **5.** b

B

1. It is a play with two actors speaking to each other. It is designed to be viewed by an audience. The words, being spoken, are open to interpretation of the actors, as well as the audience. These things do not apply, usually, to the other two texts.
(1 mark for each difference)

2. The writer can develop a third person overview, considering a range of characters. The writer can use the voice of the narrator to comment on the characters, either directly or by implying certain ideas.
(1 mark for each advantage)

C

1. A variety of answers is possible. One possible suggestion for how this might be answered:

Quotation from extract 1 – ROMEO *(Aside)* Shall I hear more, or shall I speak at this? (Romeo speaks to himself and asks questions to show his nerves and doubt at how Juliet might respond)

Quotation from extract 2 – Anxious and uneasy, the period which passed in the drawing-room, before the gentlemen came, was wearisome and dull to a degree that almost made her uncivil. (The writer uses the underlined adjectives to show Elizabeth's mood before speaking to Mr Darcy.)

Quotation from extract 3 – I dare not gaze upon her face/But left her memory in each place; (The writer uses lists of confessions in short, simple sentences to show how simple but difficult it is to show his feelings.)
(1 mark for each quotation and 1 mark for each supporting explanation)

Module 6: Poetic conventions – rhythm and rhyme (pages 25–27)

A

1. a **2.** b **3.** c **4.** b **5.** c **6.** a **7.** b

B

1. Increasing the pace – he uses a triple rhyme – ermine/determine/vermin – this speeds things up because it changes from every other line rhyming, to every line rhyming, so the rhyme words happen sooner.

Affecting the tone – The first two lines "At last the people in a body/ To the Town hall came flocking" uses enjambement/run-on lines to create a factual tone before the rush of complaints that come afterwards. The answer for "Increasing the pace" could also be used for this as the mood gets angrier through the triple rhyme.
(1 mark for each quotation and 1 mark for each supporting explanation)

2. The rhyming couplet sums up the events of the verse *(1 mark)* and also acts as a contrast between the complaints of the Hamelin people and reaction of the council members *(1 mark)*.

C

1. Various answers and several quotations possible – likely comments might include – triple rhymes and rhyming couplets make it easier to guess what is coming next/easier to follow the storyline/rhymes help to create humour or surprise, which appeals to children. Is similar to some nursery rhymes. Reward any quotations with examples of these rhymes. Lots of single-syllable stressed words, e.g. "They fought the dogs and killed the cats" make the poem easier to follow, as it contains less complex ideas.
(1 mark for each explanation and 1 mark for each supporting quotation)

2. Various answers possible – some suggestions – Weser, deep and wide, Washes its wall (W sounds mimic the effect of the river's slow flow)/And bit the babies in the cradles (The B sounds mimic the attack and biting of the rats)
(1 mark for each explanation and 1 mark for each supporting quotation)

WRITING
Module 7: Imaginative writing (pages 28–31)
A

1. d **2.** a **3.** c **4.** d **5.** c **6.** a **7.** b

B

1. Various answers possible. One answer given as a guide to what might be possible, but many different possibilities exist.

Bill walked **nervously** to the **ominous** door. The **solemn** house in front of him made him feel **anxious**.

Little did he know what **shocking** things lay inside, lurking **mysteriously** in the **shadowy** dark, waiting for someone like him to arrive. He **reluctantly** pushed the door open and stepped **gingerly** inside. From the darkness he heard a **wailing** sound.
(1 mark for each)

2. Various answers possible. One answer given as a guide to what might be possible, but many different possibilities exist.

Bill walked **joyfully** to the **bright** door. The **delightful** house in front of him made him feel **special**.

Little did he know what **beautiful** things lay inside, lurking **expectantly** in the **peaceful** dark, waiting for someone like him to arrive. He **excitedly** pushed the door open and stepped **boldly** inside. From the darkness he heard a **giggling** sound.
(1 mark for each)

3. Various answers possible. One answer given as a guide to what might be possible, but many different possibilities exist.

Bill walked **cheerily** to the **shiny** door. The **cosy** house in front of him made him feel **secure**.

Little did he know what **glorious** things lay inside, lurking **welcomingly** in the **lessening** dark, waiting for someone like him to arrive. He **quickly** pushed the door open and stepped **confidently** inside. From the darkness he heard a **sweet** sound.

(1 mark for each)

C

1. Various alternatives are possible. Check that the finished version has all the criteria given in the task. If any are missing, it should be re-written in order to improve and include those that are missing. Identify any of the criteria that you find difficult to include and revisit those sections of the Revision Guide.
(1 mark for fulfilling each point of the brief)

Module 8: Formal writing (pages 32–35)
A

1. b **2.** c **3.** a **4.** c **5.** c **6.** c **7.** c

B

1. There are various ways that this might be done – the example is given only as a guide. Check your answer against the criteria for formal letters in the Revision Guide and amend any missing or incorrect features.

Dear Mr Smith,

I would like to formally apologise for the fact that I was unable to attend the lunch appointment last Friday. Urgent family commitments that required my attention meant that I unfortunately had to re-arrange my schedule for that day.

I attempted to inform you by telephone but was unable to speak to you directly, so please accept this letter by way of formal apology. Would it be possible to re-schedule our meeting for a later date? Please contact me through the usual channels if this is possible.

Mr W. Jones

Company Director

(1 mark for a suitable attempt which contains all the information used in the original)

C

1. Various alternatives are possible. Check that the finished version has all the criteria given in the task. If any are missing, it should be re-written in order to improve and include those that are missing. Identify any of the criteria that you find difficult to include and revisit those sections of the Revision Guide.
(1 mark for fulfilling each point of the brief for layout and style. 2 marks for including all the content information; 1 mark if some of the content information is missing)

Module 9: Organising writing (pages 36–39)
A

1. a **2.** d **3.** c **4.** c **5.** d **6.** a **7.** d

B

1.

Paragraph topics – in order
Set the scene for the story
Bring first character into the scene
First character finds mysterious object
Mysterious object gives off deadly ray
Deadly ray stuns first character

(1 mark for each)

2.

Paragraph topics – in order
Explain ingredients needed for recipe
Explain how ingredients are to be prepared
Explain how ingredients are cooked
Explain, while ingredients are cooking, how dishes need to be warmed ready for fully cooked ingredients
Explain how cooked ingredients need to be presented on warmed dishes

(1 mark for each)

3.

Paragraph topics – in order
Opening salutation for the letter
Paragraph stating the purpose of writing
Paragraph developing the opening point
Paragraph concluding the main body of the letter
Closing for the letter

(1 mark for each)

C

1. Various alternatives are possible. Check that the finished version has all the criteria given in the task. If any are missing, it should be re-written in order to improve and include those that are missing. Identify any of the criteria that you find difficult to include and revisit those sections of the Revision Guide.
(1 mark for each planning method suitably completed)

Module 10: Choosing written forms – audience and purpose (pages 40–43)
A

1. c **2.** b **3.** c **4.** b **5.** a **6.** a **7.** d

B

1. Various answers possible. Examples given as suggestions of likely responses.

Formal	Would you do me the honour of going shopping with me?
Informal	Will you come shopping with me?
Formal	Henceforth I shall be known as Ernest Tubb.
Informal	I'll be called Ernest Tubb, from now on.
Formal	Would you deny me the opportunity to visit my mother?
Informal	Would you stop me from seeing my mum?
Formal	The accommodation would have benefited from sanitary improvement.
Informal	The rooms needed better toilets.
Formal	I would like to request that you desist.
Informal	Will you please stop?

(1 mark for each)

2. Various answers possible. Example given as a suggestion of a possible response.

   Hi! – Cor blimey! – have you heard about Jack? He was as daft as a soggy brush at that party on Friday. I'm not bothered if he spoke a load of twaddle about you, but he'd better not have said anything about me! The mind boggles – crikey…Speak to you about it later.

   Bye bye for now

   PS – Did he really wear a green dickie bow? You've gotta be joking?
   (1 mark for each word/phrase used)

C

1 and 2.

Various alternatives are possible. Check that the finished versions have all the criteria given in the tasks. If any are missing, they should be re-written in order to improve and include those that are missing. Identify any of the criteria that you find difficult to include and revisit those sections of the Revision Guide.

(1 mark for including each of the criteria)

Module 11: Non-narrative texts (pages 44–45)

A

1. c **2.** b **3.** c **4.** a **5.** d

B

1.

1	Cats
2	Chickens
3	Dogs
4	Elephants
5	Lions
6	Lizards
7	Sparrows
8	Tigers
9	Vultures

(1 mark for each in the correct order)

C

1. Various alternatives are possible. Check that the finished version has all the criteria given in the task. If any are missing, it should be re-written in order to improve and include those that are missing. Identify any of the criteria that you find difficult to include and revisit those sections of the Revision Guide.

   (1 mark for fulfilling each point of the brief)

Module 12: Making notes (pages 46–49)

A

1. d **2.** c **3.** c **4.** b **5.** a **6.** d **7.** d

B

1. Various alternatives are possible.
   (1 mark for each point)

2. Various alternatives are possible.
   (1 mark for a suitable mind-map)

C

1. Various alternatives are possible. Example given is just one suggested way of answering the question.

   Photography was not always seen as art, unlike now. Nineteenth-century experiments originally used chemicals to record images onto paper. In France in the 1830s J.N. Niépce used an early camera with pewter plates and bitumen. His images didn't fade – for the first time in history. Niépce and Daguerre invented the Daguerreotype using silver and iodine vapour. Plates had to be exposed for up to 15 minutes. Daguerreotypes were replaced by emulsion plates which only needed 2–3 second exposures – better for both model and photographer. Dry plates were then invented which allowed images to be stored and used later. They also meant smaller cameras could be used. This was when photography took off worldwide as it became more convenient to use.

   (5 marks for a suitable summary of 120–130 words; 4 marks for a suitable summary of 131–170 words; 3 marks for a suitable summary of 171–200 words; 2 marks for a suitable summary of 201–235 words; 1 mark for a suitable summary of 236–245 words)

Module 13: Crafting writing – openings, middles and endings (pages 50–51)

A

1. c **2.** d **3.** b **4.** c

B

1 and 2.

Various alternatives are possible. Check that the finished version has all the criteria given in the task. If any are missing, it should be re-written in order to improve and include those that are missing. Identify any of the criteria that you find difficult to include and revisit those sections of the Revision Guide.

(5 marks for task 1 completed in full. 1 mark for each step in task 2)

C

1. Various alternatives are possible. Check that the finished version has all the criteria given in the task. If any are missing, it should be re-written in order to improve and include those that are missing. Identify any of the criteria that you find difficult to include and revisit those sections of the Revision Guide.

   (1 mark for each of the criteria included in the correct paragraph)

Module 14: Drafting, editing and proofreading (pages 52–55)

A

1. a **2.** a **3.** b **4.** b

B

1. **a)** Various alternatives are possible, but the paragraph should be similar to this.

   In 1625, Charles I became king of England and married Henrietta Maria – a French, Bourbon, Roman Catholic – which upset many people. On 5 May 1640, Charles dissolved the Short Parliament, which also outraged some of his subjects. A couple of years later, in 1642, Sir John Hotham refused to let the King enter Kingston upon Hull. On 27 January 1649, Charles I's death warrant was signed and three days later he was beheaded. An Act of Parliament was passed banning anyone from being King of England. One week later on 7 February 1649, the Rump Parliament voted to abolish the English monarchy.
   (1 mark for each note included in chronological order)

   b) Various alternative wordings possible, but the answers should contain the following:

   Causes of the English Civil War
   The marriage of Charles to a French Roman Catholic princess was unpopular in 1625.

Charles dissolves the Short Parliament in 1640.

Sir John Hotham refuses to let Charles enter Kingston upon Hull in 1642.

Effects of the English Civil War

Charles was beheaded in January 1649.

An Act of Parliament was passed banning anyone from being King of England.

In 1649 the Rump Parliament voted to abolish the English monarchy.

(1 mark for each note included the appropriate paragraph)

C

1 and 2.

Various alternatives are possible. Check that the finished version has all the criteria given in the task. If any are missing, it should be re-written in order to improve and include those that are missing. Identify any of the criteria that you find difficult to include and revisit those sections of the Revision Guide.

(1 mark for task 1 completed in full. 1 mark for including each of the criteria in task 2)

GRAMMAR AND VOCABULARY

Module 15: Spelling (pages 56–57)

A

1. c **2.** c **3.** a **4.** a **5.** d

B

1. Various answers possible. Suggestions given.

  a) Acceptable – All Cowardly Custards Eat Peas Terribly And Break Lovely Eggs

  b) Embarrass – Every Member Brings A Rock Record And Suddenly Shakes.

  c) Gauge – Guess And Understand Great Efforts.

  d) Lightning – Lice Infect Glittery Hamsters Then Nearly Insult Nasty Gerbils

  e) Biased – Big Ian Ate Sausages Every day

  (1 mark for each)

2.

Word	Root
pedal	ped-
biology	bio-
crustacean	crusta-
deity	dei-
chronology	chrono-
chromatic	chroma-
auditory	audio
fraternity	frater
terrain	terra

(1 mark for each)

C

1. One mark for each homophone used correctly. Use a dictionary to check the meanings of each one used.

Module 16: Punctuation 1 (pages 58–61)

A

1. c **2.** a **3.** b **4.** d **5.** c **6.** d

B

1. These are the most likely answers.

  a) Rodney played his favourite music. No-one liked it.

  b) Jasmine bought lots of new clothes. She put them in her wardrobe.

  c) The team lost. They played badly.

  d) The oil painting was valuable. It was damaged.

  e) The girls went riding. It was raining.

  f) Singing wasn't Mike's favourite activity. He got embarrassed.

  g) Shopping online is easy. You have to wait for the goods to arrive.

  h) The toys didn't work. They were brand new.

i) Alicia did her homework. She did it badly.

j) David's nephew was in a band. They were very good.

(1 mark for each)

C

1.

	Punctuation mark	Name
1	;	Semi-colon
2	/	Forward slash/Forward stroke
3	?	Question mark
4	,	Comma
5	...	Ellipsis
6	!	Exclamation mark
7	'	Apostrophe/Raised comma
8	:	Colon
9	( )	Brackets
10	" "	Inverted commas/Speech marks/ Quotation marks

(1 mark for each)

2. Various alternatives are possible. Check that the finished version has all the criteria given in the task. If any are missing, it should be re-written in order to improve and include those that are missing. Identify any of the criteria that you find difficult to include and revisit those sections of the Revision Guide.

(1 mark for using each of the punctuation marks as required)

Module 17: Punctuation 2 (pages 62–63)

A

1. c **2.** c **3.** b **4.** c **5.** c

B

1.

Sentence	Correct use of the apostrophe	Incorrect use of the apostrophe
Joanna baked cookies but couldn't make trifle.	✓	
Tom was'nt watching carefully.		✓
Tara di'dnt get it right.		✓
Jay-Elle couldn't understand why her CD player had broken.	✓	
Ed shouldn't have plugged the wire into the wrong plug.	✓	

(1 mark for each)

C

1. A good answer (9–12 marks) will use a range of sentence types in each paragraph for different effects.

An average answer (5–8 marks) will use a lesser range of sentence types and won't always create many effects, or successful effects.

A lower than average answer (up to 4 marks) will use similar sentence types and create few effects on the reader.

Module 18: Sentences and grammar 1 (pages 64–65)

A

1. a **2.** a **3.** c **4.** a **5.** b

B

1. Subordinate clauses underlined. Main clauses boxed

  a) Although he was very young, Grant was a great musician, who many admired.

  b) Mike loved painting because it gave him an extra income, despite his teaching job.

  c) Although his children didn't like it, Gerald's beard grew because he didn't shave.

d) Robbie wrote down all his ideas, although they were only rough, because he liked to draft.

C

First change – Reversed clauses *(1 mark)*

Second change – Split the main clause and put the subordinate clause inside it. *(1 mark)*

Some variations on these answers are possible. These are the most likely choices.

1. Despite getting triple maths homework, Kieran was smiling.
Kieran, despite getting triple Maths homework, was smiling.

2. Although Callum liked the book, Aaron didn't.
Aaron, although Callum did, didn't like the book.

3. Regardless of the fact that it was cold, Ali ate his tea.
Ali, regardless of the fact that it was cold, ate his tea.

4. Because Melanie had given her germs, Sarah coughed.
Sarah, because Melanie had given her germs, coughed.

5. As a result of Dan's overpoweringly smelly socks, Ryan couldn't speak properly.
Ryan, as a result of Dan's overpoweringly smelly socks, couldn't speak properly.

6. Even though she laughed at him when he did, Danesh enjoyed tormenting Beth.
Danesh, even though she laughed at him when he did, enjoyed tormenting Beth.

7. While Charlotte bit the apples, Anthony chewed them.
Anthony, while Charlotte bit the apples, chewed them.

Module 19: Sentences and grammar 2 (pages 66–67)

A

1. b **2.** b **3.** b **4.** c **5.** b

B

1. Various answers are possible. One answer for each, given as a guide to what might be possible, but many different possibilities exist.

   a) Over and under, rumbling across the desert, they stormed and raced until they caught sight of a group of distant figures glittering in the desert twilight.

   b) Insert the diced meat into the skin, along with the diced peppers, because that is what gives the boudin sausage its flavour.

   c) Before she could turn on the light, a thin, plaintive whine pierced the darkness, sending her into a state of paralysis.

   d) Because I care, and because I mean to do what I say, I will tell you about all the good things that will come to pass if you listen to me and vote for my ideas in the forthcoming election.

   e) Multiple random entries will increase your chances of winning the lottery because the odds will change in your favour, quite unusually.

C

1. Various alternatives are possible. Check that the finished version has all the criteria given in the task. If any are missing, it should be re-written in order to improve and include those that are missing. Identify any of the criteria that you find difficult to include and revisit those sections of the Revision Guide.
(1 mark for each of the criteria included in the correct paragraphs)

SPOKEN ENGLISH

Module 20: Differences between written and spoken English (pages 68–69)

A

1. c **2.** c **3.** d **4.** c **5.** b

B

1. Various alternatives are possible. The example below is intended as a guide to a likely answer.

JESS Hello – How are you?
TOM I feel that I am alright. Are you going to visit the town tomorrow?
JESS Maybe.
TOM I thought that you would be looking forward to it.

JESS I do not know.
TOM What is the matter?
JESS Nothing is the matter. I just cannot be bothered.
(1 mark for each line of the script suitably re-written in more formal English)

C

1. Various alternatives are possible. Check that the finished version fulfils the criteria given in the task. If any are missing, it should be re-written in order to improve and include those that are missing.
(1 mark for each set of instructions suitably completed)

Module 21: Standard English, accent and dialect (pages 70–71)

A

1. d **2.** b **3.** a **4.** c **5.** d

B

1.

Geordie phrase	Translation
1	4
2	1
3	5
4	3
5	2

(1 mark for each)

C

1. Various alternatives are possible. Examples include:
Word / Phrase: LOL   Definition: "Laugh out loud" – used to show humorous approval but occasionally used in speech sarcastically.
Word / Phrase: Laters   Definition: "See you later"
(1 mark for each word/phrase and accompanying definition)

Module 22: Speeches and presentations (pages 72–73)

A

1. b **2.** b **3.** c **4.** c **5.** b

B

1. Various alternatives are possible. Examples are given to give an idea of what might be used.

Speech task	Possible props to help deliver the speech
Persuade your classmates to take part in a 50-mile sponsored charity walk.	Pictures of the charity's work. Walking shoes.
Talk about your favourite musical act.	CDs, posters, memorabilia
Talk about the best holiday that you have ever had.	Postcards, souvenirs, pictures

(1 mark for each prop)

C

1. Various alternatives are possible. For example:
Boys and girls, *(Look up and make eye-contact)*. I speak to you today to talk about not one – not two – but three *(Pound the table for emphasis)* important things. Firstly, there is the alarming issue of litter in the school playground. It's disgusting! When are students at this school going to become responsible and put their litter in the bins provided? Can you *(Point)* honestly say that you always do that? *(Shrug your shoulders)*. Secondly – and leading on from that, there is the matter of the vending machines on the corridors. They must go *(Raise volume to emphasise a point)*. I know that people will say that they are a great facility and a fund-raiser for the school, but the number of problems that they create is ridiculous! Litter! Children late for lessons! Mess! Finally, I want you to think for a moment. We are an eco-school. We should be recycling our litter.

Do we do this? *(Pause after a rhetorical question)*. Do we do our bit in helping to save the planet? I don't think we do enough *(Lower volume to get the audience to listen carefully)*.

(1 mark for each performance technique included in the speech)

TEST-STYLE PAPER
Section A – Shakespeare
Romeo and Juliet mark scheme
Find the category that best fits your answer and for every bullet point in that category that you achieve, give yourself one mark. For example, if you think you are in the 10–12 mark category and you have done two of the bullet points, then you should give yourself 11.

(1, 2 or 3 marks)
- A few simple facts and opinions about these extracts.
- There may be some misunderstandings.
- Parts of the extracts are retold or copied and answers may be only partly relevant.

(4, 5 or 6 marks)
- Contains a little explanation, showing some awareness of the needs of the question.
- Comments are relevant but are mostly about the plot.
- Some broad references to how the characters speak or act.

(7, 8 or 9 marks)
- Some general understanding of the question, although some points might not be developed.
- Some comments on the language that the characters use or the effect of the plot on the audience.
- Some points backed up with reference to the text.

(10, 11 or 12 marks)
- Some discussion of how the extracts relate to the question, even though all the ideas might not be of equal quality.
- Awareness of the characters' use of language and its effects
- Most points backed up with references to the text.

(13, 14 or 15 marks)
- Clear focus on how the extracts relate to the question.
- Good consistent comments on the characters' language and its effect on the audience.
- Well-chosen quotations linked together to present an overall argument.

(16, 17 or 18 marks)
- Every quotation is analysed in depth with relation to the question and there is an evaluation.
- Every quotation is commented on in terms of the language that the characters use or the difference between what they don't know and the audience does.
- Individual words are picked out of quotations and linked into the overall argument.

Useful quotations for *Romeo and Juliet*

Extract 1

ROMEO Out of her favour where I am in love.

Romeo is depressed about his love for Rosaline being unrequited.

O brawling love, O loving hate,
O anything of nothing first create!
O heavy lightness, serious vanity,
Misshapen chaos of well-seeming forms

The use of oxymorons shows how Romeo is confused

Love is a smoke made with the fume of sighs:

Romeo is acting out what he thinks a lover should do, but he has, of yet, no experience himself

In sadness, cousin, I do love a woman.

Romeo shows he still has a sense of humour

She will not stay the siege of loving terms,
Nor bide th'encounter of assailing eyes,

Romeo is frustrated that Rosaline does not love him in return

Farewell. Thou canst not teach me to forget.

Romeo is stubborn

Extract 2

Her eye discourses. I will answer it.
– I am too bold.

Romeo is anxious not to mess things up with Juliet

O that I were a glove upon that hand,
That I might touch that cheek!

Romeo displays the typically obsessive and exaggerated behaviour of a lover

O speak again, bright angel! – For thou art
As glorious to this night, being o'er my head,
As is a wingèd messenger of heaven

Romeo uses the clichéd language of love because he knows no better

Call me but love, and I'll be new-baptized.
Henceforth, I never will be Romeo.

Romeo makes strong promises, showing his innocence and strength of feeling

Section B – Reading
1. Any three of the following are acceptable. One mark each.

   King John used the country to get his own way.

   John ran the country for his own wicked ends.

   Taxes were raised.

   Rich and poor thrown off their land.

   Ordinary man's right to hunt and farm taken away.

   Hardship caused.

   Those who challenged authority hunted down and never seen again.

2. Two brief reasons for two marks, or one explained answer. Acceptable answers –

   To make sure that he wasn't found by King John's men. *(1 mark)*

   To save his life. *(1 mark)*

   To hide his father's identity from him, so that he was ignorant of who he was, if caught. *(2 marks)*

3. Any two of these acceptable answers:

   The Sheriff enjoyed working for the King.

   He was very cruel.

   He enjoyed inflicting pain.

4. One mark for each quotation and one mark for a reasonable explanation.

   Fearsome – possible quotation – "a giant of a man" – his size implies he is tough.

   Friendly – possible quotations – "rather wet giant" – this makes him seem less threatening; "Good humour to see the funny side" – his sense of humour implies that he has a friendly side.

5. Two correctly numbered paragraphs – 1 mark. All correct – 2 marks.

Paragraph description	Paragraph number
The Sheriff of Nottingham makes up a plan to trap Robin after the Sheriff realises that Robin and Marian are sympathetic to each other.	9
A conclusion to Robin's adventures.	11
A summary of some of the men who came to join Robin.	8
An account of an archery tournament that Robin was involved in.	10

6. Find the category that best fits your answer and for every bullet point in that category that you achieve, give yourself one mark. For example, if you think you are in the 4–6 mark category and you have done two of the bullet points, then you should give yourself 5.

(0–3 marks)

- Makes general comments about what Robin did.
- Makes general comments about what happened to Robin.
- Makes general comments with no quotations about how the writer describes Robin.

(4–6 marks)

- Makes some comments about what Robin did and refers to parts of the passage.
- Makes comments about what happened to Robin and backs it up with reference to the passage.
- Makes comments with some quotations about how the writer describes Robin but only makes simple comments about their effect.

(7–9 marks)

- Makes detailed comments about what Robin did and all are backed up from the passage.
- Makes detailed comments about what happened to Robin and closely links this to details in the passage.
- Makes comments with detailed analysis of quotations about how the writer uses different techniques such as adjectives, complex sentences, emotive language and heroic language to get the reader to feel sympathy for Robin.

Section C – Writing task

The 20 marks for the writing task are awarded on how well you have used the following:

- **Sentence structure/punctuation and paragraph organisation (6 marks)**
- **Composition and effect (10 marks)**
- **Spelling (4 marks)**

Find the category that best fits your answer, for each of the three sections above. If you have done most of a category, give yourself a high mark in that category. If you have only done a few things in the category, a lower mark should be awarded.

Add up your three scores to make an overall mark out of 20.

Sentence structure/punctuation and paragraph organisation

This section focuses on how you choose to organise your writing and how this contributes to its overall effect.

0 marks

Sentences are fairly simple.

Sentences are linked by simple joining words like "and" or "then".

Full-stops and capital letters are used with accuracy.

Paragraphs are used to separate the more obvious different topics given in the task.

1 or 2 marks

Sentences are varied and use linking words like "who" or "which". The writing is written in the same tense throughout.

Words like "He" "She" "It" "They" and other pronouns are generally used correctly.

Paragraphs are mainly put into a logical order, as is the detail within them.

3 or 4 marks

A variety of longer sentences are used. This includes those that have been built up from joining simpler ones together to make longer ones and sentences where the word order has been successfully re-arranged for effect.

Words like "Completely" "Partly" and others which help to make meaning more precise, are used.

Words like "He" "She" "It" "They" and other pronouns are used correctly.

Tenses are used correctly.

Paragraphs are used for appropriate reasons and are put into a logical order.

The detail in them is put into a logical order.

5 marks

Sentences are written in a variety of ways to achieve interesting effects that suit the purpose of the writing.

A range of punctuation is used – sometimes to create effects.

Paragraphs are of different lengths and the information in them is organised cleverly to suit what is being written about.

6 marks

There is a wide range of sentence structures that use a sophisticated range of verbs and tenses.

Within paragraphs, the writer has used a wide range of links that are precisely and carefully chosen.

There is a very wide range of punctuation used in order to make meaning clear and create a range of effects.

Composition and effect

This section is to do with the overall impact of your writing and how well it fits the audience you are writing for.

0 marks

The writing shows some awareness of the reader.

Simple techniques, like repetition, are used.

Content is relevant to the question but might well be unevenly used.

1, 2 or 3 marks

The writing tries to interest the reader.

Some techniques, e.g. use of adjectives, are used to help writing, but they might not be very imaginative.

4, 5 or 6 marks

The writer interests the reader.

The writer is clearly aware of what type of writing he/she is doing and for whom.

The tone of the writing is consistent throughout.

7, 8 or 9 marks

The writing is well-crafted and convincing throughout.

The writer really engages the reader's interest.

There is a very good range of well-chosen details.

The viewpoint of the writer is consistent throughout.

10 marks

The writing has been done skilfully and the writer is totally in control of the writing type.

The viewpoint of the writer has been maintained throughout.

There is a strong individual style, created by a range of methods.

Spelling

This section focuses on accuracy in spelling. Choose the section that best fits the writing.

1 mark

Simple words and those with more than one or two syllables are generally accurate.

2 marks

More complicated words that fit to regular patterns and rules are generally accurate.

3 marks

Most spelling, including irregular words, is accurate.

4 marks

Virtually all spelling, including complex words that don't fit to regular rules or patterns, is correct.

C | **Your answer should respond to each of the bullet points.**

1 Write an extract from a manual about how to use some of the functions on a new smartphone. The manual is the one that comes with the phone and is aimed at general users. In the page from the manual, you should include all of the following:
➤ Sections
➤ Headings
➤ Diagrams
➤ Captions
➤ Technical language/terminology
➤ Extra examples of the basic functions
➤ Detailed explanations of one or two key features

Write your answer below. (7 marks)

Score /7

For more help on this topic see KS3 English Revision Guide pages 44–47.

A **Choose just one answer, a, b, c or d.**

1 Which of these is **not** a way of shortening your ideas in note form? (1 mark)
a) abbreviations
b) letter-number homophones
c) shorthand
d) full sentences

2 Which of these is **not** a particularly useful stationery item for making notes? (1 mark)
a) highlighter pen
b) sticky notes
c) compass
d) pack of different coloured pens

3 Which of these is **not** a practical reason to put a title and date on your notes? (1 mark)
a) it will help you to sort the order of all your notes
b) it will help you to remember which notes are which
c) it will stop you getting told off by your teacher
d) it will help you to organise your notes by topic

4 Which of these is **not** a practical reason to colour-code notes made while reading? (1 mark)
a) you can organise ideas easily by theme or topic
b) your notes will look pretty
c) you will be able to quickly identify key issues or ideas
d) you will be able to associate ideas with colours as a memory aid

5 Why is it better to write in short sentences or phrases while listening and making notes? (1 mark)
a) you won't have time to write every word down
b) other people will understand what you have put
c) you might not understand everything written in full
d) other people will tell you what you have missed

6 Which of these might you do after making initial notes? (1 mark)
a) re-write them more neatly
b) colour-code them
c) reorganise them in a more useful manner
d) all three

7 Why should you ask permission if recording someone speaking? (1 mark)
a) their ideas may be copyrighted
b) they might not like the idea of being recorded
c) it is good manners
d) all three

Score /7

Answer these questions.

1 Write what you did yesterday as a series of ten bullet points. (10 marks)

1. ....

2. ....

3. ....

4. ....

5. ....

6. ....

7. ....

8. ....

9. ....

10. ....

2 Write what you did yesterday as a mind-map, in the space below. (1 mark)

Score /11

C Answer this question.

1 Read this passage and then write a full-sentence summary of it, in approximately half as many words. (5 marks)

Photography is an art form that was not originally considered an art form. In the nineteenth century, early experiments were made to try to record visual images onto paper, using a variety of chemical processes. Photography, as we would call it, began in the late 1830s in France when Joseph Nicéphore Niépce used a portable camera device to expose a pewter plate coated with bitumen to light. This is the first recorded image that did not fade and was preserved. This experiment led to collaboration between Niépce and a man named Daguerre that resulted in the creation of a process called the "Daguerreotype". A copper plate was coated with silver and exposed to iodine vapour before it was exposed to light. To create the image on the plate, the earlier Daguerreotypes had to be exposed to light for up to 15 minutes. The Daguerreotype was quite widely used until it was replaced in the late 1850s by emulsion plates, which were less expensive than Daguerreotypes and only needed 2–3 seconds of exposure time, which made it easier for action to be frozen – models didn't have to sit still for quite so long as before, which was very convenient for both photographer and model. Following this, the next innovation was the introduction of dry plates, which allowed images to be stored to be used later. Also, they meant that smaller cameras could be used. In the twentieth century, this eventually led to mass-market small cameras and the beginnings of the global phenomenon that is photography today. (257 words)

Write your answer on the next page.

Aim for 120–130 words.

For more help on this topic see KS3 English Revision Guide pages 48–51.

A Choose just one answer, a, b, c or d.

1 Which opening sentence does **not** use adjectives to grab the reader's attention? (1 mark)
a) His dark, greasy Elvis-like hair was shadowed against the café window.
b) Her shiny, glossy lipstick shimmered in the neon gloom.
c) He walked jauntily and arrogantly towards the door.
d) Their old, decrepit car shuddered and stopped.

2 Which opening sentence does **not** use adverbs to grab the reader's attention? (1 mark)
a) Joyfully, she hugged her father as he raced through the door.
b) He shrugged miserably at the fact that he had to do another test.
c) He flipped through his notes carefully to find the key to the mystery.
d) His swift movements deceived the intruder.

3 Which sentence from the middle of a set of instructions does **not** use imperatives? (1 mark)
a) Remove the cling-film and empty the contents into a heated dish.
b) Why is this happening?
c) Take care when opening the oven door as steam may issue from the pot.
d) Simmer the soup for five minutes over a low heat.

4 Which of these sentences from the middle of a story does **not** use alliteration? (1 mark)
a) The damp, dark cave interior created chills.
b) She walked over to the rusting railway track.
c) Their moment was now…
d) Tiny, tingling sensations shot through their fingers.

Score /4

B Answer these questions.

1 Write the next paragraph which follows this opening of a science fiction story, in a similar style. (5 marks)

The Robocopter beeped and glowed as it set off with a lazy humming from the Robopad. Below her, Elvira could see the lights of the city – light trails of heli-cars whizzed through the grid pattern of the streets like automated fireflies. Up ahead, she could see the approaching floating bulk of the Mars cruiser that she was going to spend the next six months on as a crew member.

....

....

....

....

....

2 Write the next five steps in this set of instructions, in a similar style. (5 marks)

How to work your electronic toy car
➤ Take all the items out of the packaging.
➤ Make sure that the battery, which is sealed in plastic, has all plastic removed.
➤ Insert the battery with the terminals facing towards the metal strips.
➤ Close the battery container.

1. ....

2. ....

3. ....

4. ....

5. ....

Score /10

C **Answer this question on a separate sheet of paper.**

1 Write three paragraphs of your own from a short story – the opening, one paragraph from the middle and a final paragraph – using the techniques listed below, as a minimum. You can use any other appropriate techniques too. The subject matter can be your own choice, but it should try to entertain the reader. (21 marks)

Opening paragraph	Middle paragraph	Closing paragraph
Adjectives	Adjectives	Ellipsis
Adverbs	Adverbs	Rhetorical questions
Alliteration	Alliteration	Adjectives
Sibilance	Sibilance	Adverbs
Simple sentences	Simple sentences	Simple sentences
Compound sentences	Compound sentences	Compound sentences
Complex sentences	Complex sentences	Complex sentences

Score /21

For more help on this topic see KS3 English Revision Guide pages 52–55.

A Choose just one answer, a, b, c or d.

1 Which of these choices contains an incorrect spelling? (1 mark)
- **a)** The singer sang the song beatifully.
- **b)** The singer sang the song badly.
- **c)** The singer sang the song beautifully.
- **d)** The singer sang the song wonderfully.

2 Which of these choices is correct? (1 mark)
- **a)** Their new house is amazing.
- **b)** There new house is amazing.
- **c)** They're new house is amazing.
- **d)** Thare new house is amazing.

3 Which of these choices contains incorrect punctuation? (1 mark)
- **a)** "How are you?" asked Fred.
- **b)** "Where are you going"? asked Samantha.
- **c)** "Who do you think you are?" shouted the man.
- **d)** "Where do we go next?" asked the driver.

4 Which of these choices contains correct punctuation? (1 mark)
- **a)** The boy ran to the shops but he walked back.
- **b)** The boy ran to the shops, but he walked back.
- **c)** The girl ate her tea but didnt drink her milk.
- **d)** The girl ate her tea; but didnt drink her milk.

Score /4

B Answer these questions.

1 Underneath are some notes that a student has made. For their History homework, they need to write them up as a draft account of the events of the English Civil War, but they are not sure whether to write the ideas up chronologically – in the order in which they happened – or to group similar ideas together, for example, causes and effects.

Using the notes, write both drafts.

1625 – Charles I of England becomes King of England and marries a French, Bourbon, Roman Catholic princess, Henrietta Maria, which upsets some people.

7 February 1649 – The Rump Parliament votes to abolish the English monarchy.

30 January 1649 – Charles I of England executed by beheading – the Rump Parliament passes an Act of Parliament banning any person from being King of England.

April 1642 – Sir John Hotham refuses the King entrance to Kingston upon Hull.

27 January 1649 – The death warrant of Charles I of England is signed.

5 May 1640 – Charles dissolves the Short Parliament, which outrages some of his subjects.

a) Write the notes up in a paragraph, in which the ideas are put in chronological order. (6 marks)

....

....

....

....

....

....

....

....

b) Write the notes up in two paragraphs entitled "Causes of the English Civil War" and "Effects of the English Civil War". (6 marks)

Paragraph 1 – "Causes of the English Civil War"

....

....

....

....

Paragraph 2 – "Effects of the English Civil War"

....

....

....

....

....

Score   /12

C Answer these questions.

1 For this, you will need something to keep time. Write as much as you can, in three minutes, about something that means a lot to you, in the space below. Stop after three minutes or when you have filled the space. *(1 mark)*

2 Now re-write what you have written in question 1. Before you do so, check if you have included the features in the table below. If you have included them already, you don't need to change what you have written. If you haven't, you need to re-draft it so that you have done. (6 marks)

| Alliteration | A complex sentence that starts with "Because" | A rhetorical question |
| A quotation, using inverted commas | At least one adjective | At least one adverb |

Score /7

For more help on this topic see KS3 English Revision Guide pages 56–59.

A — Choose just one answer, a, b, c or d.

1 Which of these is the correct spelling? (1 mark)
- a) bizness ◯
- b) busness ◯
- c) business ◯
- d) bisness ◯

2 Which of these is the correct spelling? (1 mark)
- a) neccessary ◯
- b) necesary ◯
- c) necessary ◯
- d) nessessary ◯

3 Which of these is the correct spelling? (1 mark)
- a) accommodate ◯
- b) acomodate ◯
- c) accomodate ◯
- d) acommodate ◯

4 Which of these is the correct spelling? (1 mark)
- a) conscience ◯
- b) consience ◯
- c) conshuns ◯
- d) consciense ◯

5 Which of these is the correct spelling? (1 mark)
- a) poseshun ◯
- b) posession ◯
- c) possesion ◯
- d) possession ◯

Score   /5

B — Answer these questions. Continue on a separate sheet of paper if necessary.

1 Make up mnemonics for these commonly mis-spelled words.

a) Acceptable (1 mark)

....

b) Embarrass (1 mark)

....

c) Gauge (1 mark)

....

d) Lightning (1 mark)

....

e) Biased (1 mark)

....

2 What is the root part of each of these? There is a clue for each one to help you. Where a word has more than one root part, you are looking for the part that links to the clue.

Here is an example:

Word	Clue	Root
alternative	"other"	alter

Now complete the table.

(9 marks)

Word	Clue	Root
pedal	"foot"	
biology	"life"	
crustacean	"shell"	
deity	"god"	
chronology	"time"	
chromatic	"colour"	
auditory	"sound"	
fraternity	"brother"	
terrain	"earth"	

Score /14

C **Answer this question on a separate piece of paper.**

1 Design and write a newspaper or magazine page which includes all the following homophones, used correctly.

(18 marks)

affect	effect
pour	paw
so	sew
hare	hair
bare	bear
plain	plane
here	hear
there	their
meet	meat

Score /18

For more help on this topic see KS3 English Revision Guide pages 60–63.

| A | Choose just one answer, a, b, c or d. |

1 Which of these has the full stops in the correct places? (1 mark)

a) The captain spoke to the crew he told them that all was well.
b) The captain spoke. To the crew he told them that all was well.
c) The captain spoke to the crew. He told them that all was well.
d) The captain spoke to the crew he told them. That all was well.

2 Which of these has the full stops in the correct places? (1 mark)

a) Vicky got in touch with a long-lost friend. She hadn't seen him for years.
b) Vicky got in touch. With a long-lost friend she hadn't seen him for years.
c) Vicky got in touch with a long-lost friend she hadn't seen. Him for years.
d) Vicky got in. Touch with a long-lost friend she hadn't seen him for years.

3 Which of these has the full stops in the correct places? (1 mark)

a) Puppies are cute they do. Make a mess though.
b) Puppies are cute. They do make a mess though.
c) Puppies are cute they do make a mess though.
d) Puppies are cute they do makes. A mess though.

4 Which of these has the full stops in the correct places? (1 mark)

a) The volcano erupted lava. Shot out into the sky.
b) The volcano. Erupted lava shot out into the sky.
c) The volcano erupted lava shot. Out into the sky.
d) The volcano erupted. Lava shot out into the sky.

5 Which of these has the full stops in the correct places? (1 mark)

a) The band came from Melbourne. In Australia Melbourne in Australia is well-known for producing good bands.
b) The band. Came from Melbourne in Australia. Melbourne in Australia is well-known for producing good bands.
c) The band came from Melbourne in Australia. Melbourne in Australia is well-known for producing good bands.
d) The band came from Melbourne in Australia Melbourne. In Australia is well-known for producing good bands.

6 Which of these has the full stops in the correct places? (1 mark)

a) The boy signed up for a social media website he created a secure password.
b) The boy signed up. For a social media website he created a secure password.
c) The boy signed up for a social media. Website he created a secure password.
d) The boy signed up for a social media website. He created a secure password.

Score /6

Answer all parts of the question.

1 Here are some sentences which have been joined by a connective. Take out the connective and make them into two separate sentences, using a full stop. (10 marks)

Example – Johnny went to the restaurant and ate lots of food.

Answer – Johnny went to the restaurant. He ate lots of food.

a) Rodney played his favourite music, but no-one liked it.

....

b) Jasmine bought lots of new clothes and put them in her wardrobe.

....

c) The team lost because they played badly.

....

d) The oil painting was valuable despite being damaged.

....

e) The girls went riding although it was raining.

....

f) Singing wasn't Mike's favourite activity because he got embarrassed.

....

g) Shopping online is easy, but you have to wait for the goods to arrive.

....

h) The toys didn't work despite being brand new.

....

i) Alicia did her homework but did it badly.

....

j) David's nephew was in a band, and they were very good.

....

Score   /10

C **Answer these questions.**

1 Name the following punctuation marks. (10 marks)

	Punctuation mark	Name
1	;	
2	/	
3	?	
4	,	
5	…	
6	!	
7	'	
8	:	
9	( )	
10	" "	

2 Now write a passage of your own, in which you use all the punctuation in the chart above. (10 marks)

Write an account of what happened the last time you met one of your friends.

Use Numbers 1, 3, 4, 7, 8 and 10 three or more times.

Use 2, 5, 6 and 9 once each.

Score   /20

A   Choose just one answer, a, b, c or d.

1 Which of these uses the apostrophe correctly? *(1 mark)*
a) Paul did'nt play properly. ◯
b) Stuart could'nt play his broken harmonica. ◯
c) Craig wasn't listening. ◯
d) Chris should'nt play the drums because he gets tired. ◯

2 Which of these uses the apostrophe incorrectly? *(1 mark)*
a) Sarah's cakes were famous throughout France. ◯
b) David's musicianship was outstanding. ◯
c) Vincents' violin was in tune. ◯
d) Wilson's keyboards cost a lot. ◯

3 Which of these uses the apostrophe correctly? *(1 mark)*
a) Ians' commentary was useful to the listeners. ◯
b) Alan's suit was the smartest. ◯
c) Dave ate his bean's every day. ◯
d) John had grown several moustache's over the years. ◯

4 Which of these uses the apostrophe incorrectly? *(1 mark)*
a) Johnny played his friend's guitar. ◯
b) Douglas didn't want the fun to end. ◯
c) No-one but Tommy ate the pie's. ◯
d) Joseph had a singing voice like an angel's. ◯

5 Which of these uses the apostrophe correctly? *(1 mark)*
a) The gates' to the school were closed. ◯
b) There was no-one to eat the left-over meals'. ◯
c) "Let's get there!" ◯
d) The pirates' enjoyed the treasure that they stole. ◯

Score   /5

B   Answer this question.

1 Fill in the table to indicate whether the apostrophe is in the right place or not. The first one is done for you as an example. *(5 marks)*

Sentence	Correct use of the apostrophe	Incorrect use of the apostrophe
Kurt did'nt understand.		✓
Joanna baked cookies but couldn't make trifle.		
Tom was'nt watching carefully.		
Tara di'dnt get it right.		
Jay-Elle couldn't understand why her CD player had broken.		
Ed shouldn't have plugged the wire into the wrong plug.		

Score   /5

C **Answer this question.**

1 Write a short account of a day in the life of a pound coin. Write five paragraphs. Each paragraph should include simple, compound and complex sentences. These sentences should be varied for effect, for example, to build up tension, to create humour, etc.

The first paragraph has been started for you.

It was dark and quiet in the pocket of his jeans. Suddenly, without warning, I felt them shake violently and realised that he was putting his trousers on. I banged against some ten pence pieces in the seam of the jeans pocket. (Continue the story from here)   (12 marks)

....

....

....

....

....

....

....

....

....

....

....

....

....

....

....

Score **/12**

For more help on this topic see KS3 English Revision Guide pages 68–71.

A · Choose just one answer, a, b, c or d.

1 Which of these sentences contains only one clause? (1 mark)
   a) Sam attended the Manchester Christmas market.
   b) Claire ate the cake but didn't like it.
   c) Samya served the dinner and did it very well.
   d) Ryan played mandolin but wasn't an expert.

2 Which of these sentences has more than one clause? (1 mark)
   a) Jeff read off the chart and had his eyesight tested.
   b) Tom scored an amazing, fantastic goal.
   c) Doug ran around extremely quickly.
   d) Deborah emigrated to distant New Zealand.

3 Which of these sentences has the main clause first? (1 mark)
   a) Before she could answer, Megan started to cry.
   b) Although she was clever, Belinda was naughty.
   c) Hannah was involved in lots of sports but still found time for drama.
   d) Despite playing for the football team, Katie did her exam very well.

4 Which of these sentences has the subordinate clause first? (1 mark)
   a) Although it rained on and off, Matt played football.
   b) Joe worked extremely hard, despite Max's behaviour.
   c) Georgia raised her hand, because she knew the answer.
   d) Anna was late, although she had left the Music room early.

5 Which of these sentences contains the most clauses? (1 mark)
   a) Alfredo never spoke but paid attention carefully.
   b) Jo-Shun worked hard because he wanted to do well and get a good job.
   c) David's dream of being a top DJ was reinforced by his desire to succeed.
   d) Lydia's sister was a professional photographic model, but not famous.

Score /5

B · Answer all parts of the question.

1 Circle the main clause and underline the subordinate clauses in each of these sentences.

   a) Although he was very young, Grant was a great musician, who many admired. (1 mark)
   b) Mike loved painting because it gave him an extra income, despite his teaching job. (1 mark)
   c) Although his children didn't like it, Gerald's beard grew because he didn't shave. (1 mark)
   d) Robbie wrote down all his ideas, although they were only rough, because he liked to draft. (1 mark)

Score /4

C	**Answer these questions by changing each sentence in two ways, to achieve different effects.**

Example: Neil was angry because he couldn't go on holiday.

First change: Reverse the clauses – Because he couldn't go on holiday, Neil was angry.

Second change: Split the main clause and put the subordinate clause inside it – Neil, because he couldn't go on holiday, was angry.

1 Kieran was smiling despite getting triple Maths homework. (2 marks)

2 Aaron didn't like the book, although Callum did. (2 marks)

3 Ali ate his tea regardless of the fact that it was cold. (2 marks)

4 Sarah coughed because Melanie had given her germs. (2 marks)

5 Ryan couldn't speak properly as a result of Dan's overpoweringly smelly socks. (2 marks)

6 Danesh enjoyed tormenting Beth even though she laughed at him when he did. (2 marks)

7 Anthony chewed the apples while Charlotte bit them. (2 marks)

Score /14

For more help on this topic see KS3 English Revision Guide pages 72–75.

A   Choose just one answer, a, b, c or d.

1   Which of these short sentences is used to give instructions?   (1 mark)
- **a)** That is weird.
- **b)** Don't do it!
- **c)** Here we are.
- **d)** They stopped doing it.

2   Which of these short sentences is used to create shocking impact?   (1 mark)
- **a)** That is good.
- **b)** Don't go there!
- **c)** Here they are.
- **d)** They started doing it.

3   Which of these sentences is **not** a complex sentence?   (1 mark)
- **a)** Because she practised hard, she won the race.
- **b)** Andy played cricket and Sam played cricket too.
- **c)** Katie achieved her goal because she had been well prepared.
- **d)** Although she was very hard-working, Emma did not do well in exams.

4   Which of these complex sentences contains descriptive detail that is most likely to be found in a story?   (1 mark)
- **a)** Turn the dial until it reaches the centre position and then push it inwards.
- **b)** Walk along the Caledonian Canal for several miles until you come to a lock gate, and it is at this point that you should turn left.
- **c)** He turned and slid downwards, falling further into the mire of mud and undergrowth, never to reappear.
- **d)** Remove the packaging, take out the ingredients and insert in a warm dish.

5   Which of these sentences is **not** a compound sentence?   (1 mark)
- **a)** Remove the foil and eat the contents.
- **b)** Because they removed the foil, they were able to eat the contents.
- **c)** Eat the contents but don't forget to remove the foil.
- **d)** Eat the contents and remove the foil.

Score   /5

B   Answer all parts of the question.

1   Write a complex sentence for each of the following reasons.

   a) To add descriptive excitement and pace to an adventure story.   (1 mark)

....

....

b) To add detail to a set of instructions. (1 mark)

c) To create tension or suspense in a mystery story. (1 mark)

d) As part of a persuasive speech, to add authority and to create the impression that the speaker knows what they are talking about. (1 mark)

e) To develop an argument, by adding in extra information to make it seem more believable. (1 mark)

Score / 5

C **Answer this question.**

1 Below is a plan for three important parts of a short ghost story. The writer has identified where different types of sentences are needed, for different effects. Write the three important parts of the story, based on the notes given.

Opening paragraph	Climax of the story	Final paragraph
➤ Short, simple sentences to build up tension at the start. ➤ Compound sentences to create a matter of fact style about the setting. ➤ Complex sentences to set the scene.	➤ Complex sentences to build up suspense – leave the main clauses until the end of the sentences, so that tension is increased. ➤ Complex sentences also used to describe the main character's thoughts and feelings about experiencing the ghost.	➤ Use short sentences to create mystery. ➤ Use ellipses within the sentences and at the end to make the reader wonder what is going on.

Write the three paragraphs on a separate piece of paper. (7 marks)

Score /7

For more help on this topic see KS3 English Revision Guide pages 76–79.

A Choose just one answer, a, b, c or d.

1 Which of these is the odd one out? *(1 mark)*
- **a)** Moolah ☐
- **b)** Dosh ☐
- **c)** Money ☐
- **d)** Dough ☐

2 Which of these is the odd one out? *(1 mark)*
- **a)** Yer what? ☐
- **b)** Innit? ☐
- **c)** I beg your pardon? ☐
- **d)** Wassup? ☐

3 Which of these is the odd one out? *(1 mark)*
- **a)** Da bomb ☐ **b)** Brill ☐
- **c)** Fab ☐ **d)** Excellent ☐

4 Which of these is the odd one out? *(1 mark)*
- **a)** Dunna ☐
- **b)** Wunna ☐
- **c)** Do not ☐
- **d)** Shunna ☐

5 Which of these is the odd one out? *(1 mark)*
- **a)** The Slammer ☐
- **b)** Gaol/Jail ☐
- **c)** The Clink ☐
- **d)** The Joint ☐

Score /5

B Answer this question.

1 Re-write this script of a conversation between two teenage friends in more formal English. *(7 marks)*

JESS	Ay up – how're you?
TOM	OK 'spose. You going up town t'morrow?
JESS	Mebbe.
TOM	Thought you'd be well up for it?
JESS	Dunno.
TOM	Wassa matter?
JESS	Nothin' – jus' can't be bothered.

....

....

....

....

....

....

Score /7

C   Answer this question.

1 Watch and record a TV cookery programme. Select a couple of minutes of the programme where there is an explanation of how to make a dish or meal. Through watching it a few times, make a transcript of what you hear. Try to write down the important instructions as they are spoken.

Write the instructions in the space below. After that, re-write the same instructions, but this time for a cookery book.

(2 marks)

Transcript

Cookery book version

Score   /2

For more help on this topic see KS3 English Revision Guide pages 80–83.

A Choose just one answer, a, b, c or d.

1 Which of these is **not** a regional dialect? *(1 mark)*
a) Scouse ◯
b) Geordie ◯
c) Brummie ◯
d) Received pronunciation ◯

2 Which of these is the most northern dialect? *(1 mark)*
a) Estuary ◯
b) Geordie ◯
c) Cockney ◯
d) Brummie ◯

3 Which of these is the most southern dialect? *(1 mark)*
a) Estuary ◯
b) Geordie ◯
c) Potteries ◯
d) Brummie ◯

4 Which of these dialects is usually associated with rhymes? *(1 mark)*
a) Estuary ◯
b) Geordie ◯
c) Cockney ◯
d) Brummie ◯

5 Which of these is the odd one out? *(1 mark)*
a) The Queen's English ◯
b) BBC English ◯
c) Oxford English ◯
d) Standard English ◯

Score   /5

B Answer this question.

1 Below are a number of expressions written in the Geordie dialect. They are written as they sound. Match up the Geordie expressions with their translations. *(5 marks)*

Geordie phrases

1	Ye knaa what ah mean leik.
2	Gan canny or we'll dunsh summick.
3	Divvent dee that.
4	Aa'd better gan canny.
5	Thor's nowt to be afeared on.

Translations

1	Be careful or we'll crash into something.
2	There is nothing to be afraid of.
3	You had better be careful.
4	You know what, I mean like.
5	Don't do that.

Answer grid

Geordie phrase	Translation
1	
2	
3	
4	
5	

Score   /5

C | **Answer this question.**

1 An individual's own personal language is called their idiolect and the language of a group that they belong to is their sociolect. Make a list of 10 words or phrases that you use, that your parents or the older generation do not use. Write them in the table below, with definitions, to create a mini-idiolect / sociolect glossary.

(10 marks)

Word/Phrase	Definition

Score /10

For more help on this topic see KS3 English Revision Guide pages 84–87.

A — Choose just one answer, a, b, c or d.

1 Which of these is the odd one out? *(1 mark)*
- a) cue cards ◯
- b) props ◯
- c) script ◯
- d) notes ◯

2 Which of these is a good idea to engage your audience? *(1 mark)*
- a) reading slides off a board, word for word, that the audience can see ◯
- b) use props to talk about ◯
- c) speak in the same tone throughout your speech ◯
- d) speak at the same pace throughout your speech ◯

3 Which of these is the odd one out? *(1 mark)*
- a) use slang ◯
- b) tell jokes ◯
- c) address your audience in formal language throughout ◯
- d) make fun of your subject ◯

4 Which of these is the odd one out? *(1 mark)*
- a) address your audience in formal language throughout ◯
- b) maintain a mature tone ◯
- c) pull funny faces to illustrate points ◯
- d) use lots of facts and evidence ◯

5 Which of these is unlikely to be a feature of a formal speech? *(1 mark)*
- a) serious language ◯
- b) rude jokes ◯
- c) a mature tone ◯
- d) lots of facts and evidence ◯

Score /5

B — Answer this question.

1 You have been given three choices of speech topics for a school assignment. For each topic, it has been suggested that you bring in some props to help deliver the speech. Fill in the chart below and list three interesting props that you might use to help deliver each speech. *(3 marks)*

Speech task	Possible props to help deliver the speech
Persuade your classmates to take part in a 50-mile sponsored charity walk.	
Talk about your favourite musical act.	
Talk about the best holiday that you have ever had.	

Score /3

C Answer this question.

1 Write a speech of your own to persuade your classmates to support a cause that you feel strongly about. Use the performance techniques listed in the table below and then annotate your speech in the places where you are going to use each technique.

(7 marks)

Technique	Key/Colour
1. Pound the table for emphasis.	
2. Shrug your shoulders.	
3. Raise volume to emphasise a point.	
4. Pause after a rhetorical question.	
5. Look up and make eye-contact.	
6. Point.	
7. Lower volume to get the audience to listen carefully.	

When you have annotated the speech, practise delivering it, either in front of a mirror or someone you know well. Does it look natural? If it doesn't, re-draft it and try again. Repeat until you are happy with your performance.

Score /7

For more help on this topic see KS3 English Revision Guide pages 88–91.

Section A: Shakespeare

Romeo and Juliet

You should spend about 45 minutes on this section and it has 18 marks.

Romeo and Juliet

In these scenes, the audience sees Romeo in different situations.

What do we learn about Romeo in these two scenes?

Support your ideas by referring to both of the following extracts.

Extract 1

ROMEO	Ay me, sad hours seem long.	155
	Was that my father that went hence so fast?	
BENVOLIO	It was. What sadness lengthens Romeo's hours?	
ROMEO	Not having that which, having, makes them short.	
BENVOLIO	In love?	
ROMEO	Out –	160
BENVOLIO	Of love?	
ROMEO	Out of her favour where I am in love.	
BENVOLIO	Alas, that Love, so gentle in his view,	
	Should be so tyrannous and rough in proof!	
ROMEO	Alas, that Love, whose view is muffled still,	165
	Should without eyes see pathways to his will!	
	Where shall we dine? O me! What fray was here?	
	Yet tell me not, for I have heard it all.	
	Here's much to do with hate, but more with love.	
	Why then, O brawling love, O loving hate,	170
	O anything of nothing first create!	
	O heavy lightness, serious vanity,	
	Misshapen chaos of well-seeming forms!	
	Feather of lead, bright smoke, cold fire, sick health,	
	Still-waking sleep, that is not what it is!	175
	This love feel I, that feel no love in this.	
	Dost thou not laugh?	
BENVOLIO	No, coz, I rather weep.	
ROMEO	Good heart, at what?	
BENVOLIO	At *thy* good heart's oppression.	
ROMEO	Why, such is love's transgression.	
	Griefs of mine own lie heavy in my breast,	180
	Which thou wilt propagate to have it pressed	
	With more of thine. This love that thou hast shown	
	Doth add more grief to too much of mine own.	
	Love is a smoke made with the fume of sighs:	
	Being purged, a fire sparkling in lovers' eyes;	185
	Being vexed, a sea nourished with loving tears.	
	What is it else? A madness most discreet,	

	A choking gall, and a preserving sweet.	
	Farewell, my coz.	
BENVOLIO	Soft, I will go along –	
	And if you leave me so, you do me wrong.	190
ROMEO	Tut, I have lost myself. I am not here.	
	This is not Romeo: he's some other where.	
BENVOLIO	Tell me in sadness, who is that you love?	
ROMEO	What, shall I groan and tell thee?	
BENVOLIO	Groan? Why no –	
	But sadly tell me who.	195
ROMEO	Bid a sick man in sadness make his will –	
	A word ill urged to one that is so ill.	
	In sadness, cousin, I do love a woman.	
BENVOLIO	I aimed so near when I supposed you loved.	
ROMEO	A right good mark-man! And she's fair I love.	200
BENVOLIO	A right fair mark, fair coz, is soonest hit.	
ROMEO	Well, in that hit you miss. She'll not be hit	
	With Cupid's arrow. She hath Dian's wit,	
	And in strong proof of chastity well-armed,	
	From Love's weak childish bow she lives uncharmed.	205
	She will not stay the siege of loving terms,	
	Nor bide th' encounter of assailing eyes,	
	Nor ope her lap to saint-seducing gold.	
	O, she is rich in beauty – only poor	
	That when she dies, with beauty dies her store.	210
BENVOLIO	Then she hath sworn that she will still live chaste?	
ROMEO	She hath, and in that sparing makes huge waste,	
	For beauty, starved with her severity,	
	Cuts beauty off from all posterity.	
	She is too fair, too wise, wisely too fair,	215
	To merit bliss by making me despair.	
	She hath forsworn to love, and in that vow	
	Do I live dead, that live to tell it now.	
BENVOLIO	Be ruled by me: forget to think of her.	
ROMEO	O, teach me how I should forget to think!	220
BENVOLIO	By giving liberty unto thine eyes:	
	Examine other beauties.	
ROMEO	'Tis the way	
	To call hers – exquisite – in question more.	
	These happy masks that kiss fair ladies' brows,	
	Being black, puts us in mind they hide the fair.	225
	He that is strucken blind cannot forget	
	The precious treasure of his eyesight lost.	
	Show me a mistress that is passing fair:	
	What doth her beauty serve, but as a note	
	Where I may read who passed that passing fair?	230
	Farewell. Thou canst not teach me to forget.	
BENVOLIO	I'll pay that doctrine, or else die in debt.	

Exeunt.

Test-style paper

Extract 2

The garden, beside the Capulet house.
Romeo comes forward (reacting to Mercutio's joking).

ROMEO He jests at scars that never felt a wound.

(Enter Juliet, coming to her window-balcony above. Romeo,
below, sees the light at the window, then realises it is Juliet.)

– But soft! What light through yonder window breaks?
It is the east, and Juliet is the sun.
Arise, fair sun, and kill the envious moon,
Who is already sick and pale with grief   5
That thou her maid art far more fair than she.
Be not her maid, since she is envious:
Her vestal livery is but sick and green,
And none but fools do wear it. Cast it off.
– It is my lady! – O, it is my love!   10
O that she knew she were!
She speaks – yet she says nothing. What of that?
Her eye discourses. I will answer it.
– I am too bold. 'Tis not to me she speaks.
Two of the fairest stars in all the heaven,   15
Having some business, do entreat her eyes
To twinkle in their spheres till they return.
What if her eyes were there, they in her head?
The brightness of her cheek would shame those stars
As daylight doth a lamp. Her eyes in heaven   20
Would through the airy region stream so bright
That birds would sing and think it were not night!
See how she leans her cheek upon her hand.
O that I were a glove upon that hand,
That I might touch that cheek!

JULIET	Ay me!	
ROMEO *(Aside)*	She speaks	25
	O speak again, bright angel! – For thou art	
	As glorious to this night, being o'er my head,	
	As is a wingèd messenger of heaven	
	Unto the white-upturnèd wondering eyes	
	Of mortals that fall back to gaze on him	30
	When he bestrides the lazy-pacing clouds,	
	And sails upon the bosom of the air.	
JULIET	O Romeo, Romeo! Wherefore art thou Romeo?	
	Deny thy father and refuse thy name –	
	Or if thou wilt not, be but sworn my love	35
	And I'll no longer be a Capulet.	
ROMEO *(Aside)*	Shall I hear more, or shall I speak at this?	
JULIET	'Tis but thy name that is my enemy.	
	Thou art myself, though not a Montague.	
	What's 'Montague'? It is nor hand, nor foot,	40
	Nor arm, nor face, nor any other part	
	Belonging to a man. O, be some other name!	
	What's in a name? That which we call a rose	
	By any other word would smell as sweet.	
	So Romeo would, were he not Romeo called,	45
	Retain that dear perfection which he owes	
	Without that title. Romeo, doff thy name –	
	And for that name, which is no part of thee,	
	Take all myself.	
ROMEO	I take thee at thy word.	
	Call me but love, and I'll be new-baptized.	50
	Henceforth, I never will be Romeo.	

Test-style paper

Write your answer here. If you run out of space, continue on lined paper.

The Story of Robin Hood

Read the passage and answer the questions that follow.

You should spend about 30 minutes on this section. It is worth 22 marks.

Test-style paper

This story is hundreds of years old and has been passed down over generations by word of mouth and in many written down versions. The story is known in different forms in different parts of the United Kingdom and many places – especially in the Midlands and the North – claim to have a link with the story's hero. Even the name of the story's hero is not constant – but most people would know him as Robin Hood.

1

The story began around the time of the Crusades – Richard the Lionheart had left England and the country was being run by his brother, King John, who used his brother's absence to get his own way and run the country for his own wicked ends. Taxes were raised; the rich and the poor were thrown off their land and the ordinary man's right to hunt and farm was taken away. This great injustice caused incredible hardship. Anyone who sought to challenge the King's authority was hunted down and was never seen again.

2

King John had spies up and down the land and he put his own men in positions of strength and influence all over the country to take away the land and property of anyone who might be powerful enough to challenge him. One such man was the Earl of Loxley, whose lands were taken from him. Not only that, but it was believed that he was imprisoned and put to death. His son, Robin was sent away by the Earl when he knew that he was in danger. He was brought up in secrecy, safely away from his father's former land, unaware of who his father was and what had happened to him.

3

Many years went by and the boy grew into a strong youth and because he was obviously so unlike his elderly adopted parents, he began to wonder who he really was. On his death bed, his guardian told Robin all. Distressed by the death of his step-father and overcome with rage at what had happened to his real father, Robin vowed to find out to find out who was responsible and get revenge.

4

Robin wasn't very careful about keeping his ideas secret at first and King John's spies found out that there was a young man who was intent on stirring up trouble. The man who was responsible for carrying out King John's orders in the area where Robin lived was called the Sheriff of Nottingham. He was particularly ruthless in carrying out the King's wishes and had many armed men and spies who would do his bidding.

5

It wasn't long, therefore, before the Sheriff's men came looking for Robin. Luckily, Robin had been brought up amongst skilled woodsmen and he knew the ways of the forest and the places where the Sheriff's men would never find him. At that time, the forests were far bigger than they are now and Sherwood Forest was a dark and mysterious place where men could hide and, if they were careful, not get caught. Robin ran away from the Sheriff's men and hid successfully in Sherwood Forest. At first, legend has it that he hid inside a massive oak tree with a hollow centre – the Sheriff's men rode past and never suspected that he was inside.

6

In the days that followed, Robin discovered that he wasn't the only rebel taking refuge in the forests. One day, when attempting to cross a fierce stream along a fallen tree he was met face-to-face with a giant of a man. The tall man refused to move out of the way – and so did Robin. A challenge arose. Both men grabbed hold of large branches from the fallen tree and agreed to use them as weapons in the challenge that they had now set each other. The tall fellow swung for Robin first, but Robin was quick and nimble enough to dodge his attempted blow. Not only that, but as the giant of a man threw all his effort into his strike, Robin's dodge had set him off balance. Quick as a flash, Robin nudged him into the water, without the need for any great strength! Laughing, Robin gave his hand to the big, but rather wet giant and helped him over to the side of the river. Fortunately, the soggy chap had enough good humour to see the funny side of what had happened to him and he shook Robin's hand and introduced himself as John Little – Robin quickly re-christened him Little John as a result of his great size. The two became firm friends almost immediately and Robin's band of outlaw brothers was born.

7

Many other men were soon to join Robin – many men who had otherwise been of good character, but who had been persecuted by the Sheriff of Nottingham and forced to take refuge in Sherwood Forest. Among them were men whose names too became part of the Robin Hood legend – Friar Tuck, Much the Miller, Will Scarlet and many others. Apart from Will Scarlet, who liked to wear reddish-brown clothing, Robin's men wore green clothing as a form of camouflage. This became known as Lincoln green.

8

Robin and his band of outlaws swore to fight back against the evil of the Sheriff of Nottingham and King John and help the poor of the land. They undertook many raids to help the poor and needy. On one such raid, Robin came across the beautiful Maid Marian, who, being of a caring and sensitive nature herself, sympathised with Robin's mission. She was upset by the evil doings that she saw going on in the name of the King but felt powerless to do anything. She started to fall in love with Robin himself. The Sheriff of Nottingham realised this and hatched a secret plan to lure Robin into the open, where he could be captured. He organised an archery competition, with a golden arrow as its prize, to be presented by Maid Marian. Knowing that Robin would not resist the challenge, he surrounded the venue with thousands of his men, in disguise.

9

As the Sheriff suspected, Robin did turn up, heavily disguised, at the tournament. After several rounds, there was only Robin and the Sheriff's best archer left. The Sheriff's man shot a perfect shot, exactly in the middle of the bullseye. The pressure was on, with Maid Marian and the Sheriff watching and surrounded on all sides by the Sheriff's men, but Robin came good – he shot his arrow and split the Sheriff's man's arrow in two, winning the prize. As he went up to accept his golden arrow, the order was given to capture him – but Robin had out-thought the Sheriff – his men – also in disguise, leapt into the area where the Sheriff and Maid Marian were seated and held the Sheriff until Robin could get away with not only the golden arrow, but Maid Marian too...

10

This was one of many adventures that made Robin, Marian and their men into heroic figures. Eventually, King Richard escaped from his foreign prison and returned to England where he knighted Robin for what he had done and returned the Earl of Loxley's land to their rightful owner – and also carried out the wedding of Robin and Marian!

11

Read the questions carefully and write your answers in the spaces provided.

1 Give three effects of King John becoming king, from Paragraph 2.

Effect 1 ....

....

Effect 2 ....

....

Effect 3 ....

....

(3 marks)

2 In Paragraph 3, why do you think that Robin of Loxley was brought up in secrecy?

....

....

....

....

....

....

....

....

(2 marks)

3 In Paragraph 5, what does the phrase "He was particularly ruthless in carrying out the King's wishes" imply about the Sheriff of Nottingham?

....

....

....

....

....

....

....

(2 marks)

4 How does the writer make Little John seem both fearsome and friendly in Paragraph 7?

Use two quotations to support your answer, one for each feature of Little John.

Little John seems fearsome because ....

....

....

....

....

Little John seems friendly because ....

....

....

....

....

(4 marks)

5 Here is a table which gives a summary of Paragraphs 8, 9, 10 and 11. The descriptions are not in the correct order. Write the correct paragraph numbers in the boxes next to the descriptions.

Paragraph description	Paragraph number
The Sheriff of Nottingham makes up a plan to trap Robin after the Sheriff realises that Robin and Marian are sympathetic to each other.	
A conclusion to Robin's adventures.	
A summary of some of the men who came to join Robin.	
An account of an archery tournament that Robin was involved in.	

(2 marks)

6 How does the writer make the reader feel sympathy for Robin Hood in this passage?

You should comment on:
- what the writer says that Robin did
- what happened to Robin
- how the writer describes Robin and others.

Support your answer with evidence from the passage.   **(9 marks)**

Section C: Writing task

You should spend 30 minutes on this section.

> "Teenagers spend far too much time in front of the computer"
>
> Write an **opinion article** for a **local newspaper** in which you argue for **or** against this statement.
>
> The article is **mainly aimed at teenagers**, but many **older people will read it too**.

Write your answer below.   **(20 marks)**